THE SMALLER MYSTERY CARNIVORES OF THE WESTCOUNTRY

JONATHAN DOWNES

Edited by Jonathan Downes
Cover and internal design by Mark North for CFZ Communications
Using Microsoft Word 2000, Microsoft , Publisher 2000, Adobe Photoshop CS.

First published in Great Britain by CFZ Press

CFZ Press
Myrtle Cottage
Woolfardisworthy
Bideford
North Devon
EX39 5QR

© CFZ MMVI

All rights reserved. Without limiting the rights under copyright reserved above, no part of this publication may be reproduced, stored in or introduced into a retrieval system, or transmitted, in any form of by any means (electronic, mechanical, photocopying, recording or otherwise), without the prior written permission of both the copyright owners and the publishers of this book.

ISBN: 978-1-905723-05-8

*"There are Marten Cats and Badgers,
And Foxes in the Enchanted Woods".*

                W.B. Yeats: "Celtic Twilight".

For
Richard Muirhead,
and my darling Corinna

CONTENTS

Foreword by Dr. Karl P.N. Shuker	9
Introduction	11
CHAPTER ONE - THE WILDCAT	15
CHAPTER TWO - THE POLECAT	35
CHAPTER THREE - THE PINE MARTEN	53
CHAPTER FOUR - OTHER MARTEN SPECIES	77
CONCLUSION	95
APPENDIX ONE - NOTES ON THE IRISH WILDCAT	97
APPENDIX TWO - MUSTELID HYBRIDS	105
APPENDIX THREE - MAMMALS OF SOMERSET	109
APPENDIX FOUR - THE IRISH STOAT, THE PYGMY WEASEL, & MUIRHEAD'S MYSTERY MUSTELIDS	111
REFERENCES	117
ACKNOWLEDGEMENTS	125

FOREWORD

Anyone who believes that mystery animals can only be encountered in remote, faraway places or that such creatures can only be interesting if they are totally alien and spectacular, should read this book carefully and duly repent of the error of their ways.

Jonathan Downes has performed a notable service to cryptozoology in general, and British cryptozoology in particular by demonstrating that thought-provoking discoveries pertinent to this fledgling science can be made quite literally upon our own doorstep – and featuring species that may not previously have been deemed worthy of cryptozoological attention.

Nowadays, few people can be unaware that Southwestern England is prowled by a plenitude of panthers, pumas, and other feline phantasmagoria of sizeable stature. Within the pages of this new book, however, the reader will encounter a rich variety of smaller, yet no less interesting mystery carnivores reported from the Westcountry. I was especially intrigued to learn that the beech marten, a species of mustelid officially recorded only from continental Europe in historic times, may also have thrived here until quite recently. Apparently distinguished from the pine marten by local people, but remaining unrecognised by British zoologists, it eventually vanished from the records – sinking forever into the morass of scientific anonymity that has claimed many other cryptozoological victims in the past.

Everyone with an interest in mystery animals, great and small, near and far, should read *The Smaller Mystery Carnivores of the Westcountry*. Not only is it a valuable addition to the cryptozoological literature, it is a very encouraging example of how we can still make worthwhile discoveries – if we take time to look around us, and the trouble to investigate what we find.

Dr. Karl P.N. Shuker BSc PhD FRES FZS
February 1996

INTRODUCTION

'All cats are not grey after midnight-endless variety'

Lazarus Long

I am a Fortean Zoologist. [see footnote] The term is my own and describes a school of zoology which studies the animal kingdom according to precepts suggested by the American author and philosopher, Charles Fort. Fort was fascinated by Natural History as a child, but as an adult he dedicated his life to collecting and recording anomalous phenomena. He claimed the title of 'The Arch Enemy of Science', [1] because of his continual assertions that Scientists chose what knowledge to accept in order to prove their theories, instead of formulating their theories around what knowledge was available. He called this rejected knowledge 'Damned - as in Excluded'. And it is the study of this 'Damned' knowledge which has coined the adjective 'Fortean' in his honour.

The study of Unknown Animals is known as Cryptozoology. The term was first coined by Dr. Bernard Heuvelmans in a book called *On the Track of Unknown Animals*, Thirty or more years later he reiterated the aims of the science he had invented. [2]

> "The Scientific study of hidden animals, i.e. of still unknown animal forms about which only testimonial and circumstantial evidence is available, or material evidence considered insufficient by some!"

---

1. I originally wanted to call my nascent disciple `Anarchozoology`, for reasons that made great sense to me at the time. I was theorising a discipline that would do for zoology what chaos mathematics had done for sums. However, my ex-wife warned me against it, and it was probably a good idea.

Genuinely unknown animals that conform to the outlines laid out by Heuvelmans are known as 'Cryptids'. There are many other 'unknown' animals that do not fall within Heuvelmans' strict criteria. There are many reports of animals, which although they belong to a 'known' species, are found to be living in a location where, according to established thought at least, they should not be living. I have named such creatures 'Pseudocryptids'. Some of these animals may be endemic to the area in which their anomalous occurrence was reported and others may have been introduced – either accidentally or on purpose. It is the mere fact of their existence in a situation which challenges accepted scientific thought that makes them Fortean. There is a third type of phenomenon of interest to the Fortean Zoologist. These are the 'Zooform Phenomena' – things which appear to be 'flesh and blood' animals, but which further investigation proves are not 'real' at least under the terms by which we accept 'reality' as defined by conventional physics. [3]

The natural history of the British Isles, is undoubtedly better known than that of any other country in the world. Generations of enthusiastic and gifted amateurs mapped, catalogued and defined the zoofauna of Britain, until it would seem that there could be nothing left to discover. Indeed, as a child I lived in Hong Kong, one of the last of the British Crown Colonies, and a land which, although more densely populated than most other portions of the globe, still boasted small tracts of virgin forest whose denizens included such exciting beasts as porcupines and pangolins.

My family moved to England in 1971, and I found myself in a position, horrible for an eleven-year-old, of a feeling of zoological ennui. How could the Bristol Channel compare with the South China Sea? How could the fields and streams of North Devon compare with sub-tropical rain forest? When you had the entire continent of Asia as your hinterland, anything seemed possible. Through my jaded eleven-year-old eyes, it seemed like England had no animal mysteries left to solve. This, of course, was far from true.

In the mid-1970s I became aware of the burgeoning population of Himalayan porcupines that were living in Devonshire, [4][5] and a few years later the first reports of mysterious big cats on Exmoor began to appear in the press. I discovered that a family of beavers was living on the River Axe, [6] and I began to hear whispers of some strange goings on near the village of Mawnan Smith in Cornwall. [7]

I slowly began to realise that the zoological establishment has become extraordinarily complacent. What was perhaps excusable to an eleven year old with stars in his eyes is completely inexcusable in a whole breed of adult professionals. Nevertheless, the official view of the scientific 'establishment' is that the zoofauna of Great Britain is both completely known and relatively safe. My researches over the last few years have indicated that this does not seem to be the case.

- THE SMALLER MYSTERY CARNIVORES OF THE WESTCOUNTRY -

In a paper entitled *The Decline of the Rarer Carnivores in Britain*, published in the *Mammal Review* of 1977, two British zoologists, P.J.W. Langley and D.W. Yalden, described, county by county, the inexorable decline towards extinction of three native British carnivores, one felid, the wildcat (*Felis sylvestris*), and two mustelids, the pine marten (*Martes martes*) and the polecat (*Mustela putorius*). It was an excellent piece of scholarship with one important proviso – they were completely wrong! [8]

In the Southwest for example, they state that all three species are extinct, and give the following dates for the extinction:

DEVON

Polecat 1887
Pine Marten 1870 – 80
Wildcat before 1793

CORNWALL

Polecat c. 1890
Pine Marten 1879
Wildcat ?

DORSET

Polecat 1890 – 1900
Pine Marten 1800 – 50
Wildcat ?

SOMERSET

Polecat 1900 – 1910
Pine Marten 1870 – 80
Wildcat ?

These dates are all totally inaccurate. With all three species there are enough records from all over the region to suggest that they survived in the Southwest until very recently, in some cases to the present day.

Other small carnivores, whose existence is officially disputed, also live in the area. Several such species have been introduced into the area over the past centuries, and whereas it is generally accepted that several large cats, probably pumas, are living wild on Bodmin Moor and Exmoor, [9] [10] other less well-known species have also been introduced. There is even a mounting body of evidence that one species, not previously known from the British Isles, lived in the Southwest at least into historical times.

The larger mystery carnivores of the region, the Celtic Black Dogs and the Alien Big Cats, have been dealt with elsewhere in such exhaustive detail that this author cannot hope to compete. The intention of this book is to investigate these lesser known mystery animals in more depth and to discuss the implications of their existence upon the ecosystem, and upon the study of the natural sciences as a whole.

- CHAPTER ONE -
THE WILDCAT

'Never try to outstubborn a cat'.

Lazarus Long

The British race of the forest wildcat (*Felis silvestris*) was once found all over the British Isles, but according to accepted belief today, they had been exterminated over much of mainland Britain during the 17th, 18th and 19th Centuries.

As we have seen, Langley and Yalden provided scientific dates for the extermination of the creature in the four counties of the Southwestern peninsula. Recent research has thrown doubt, not only upon their findings, but also upon the status of the species as a whole.

The taxonomy of the European wildcat has long been a source of difficulty and confusion. Writing in 1758, in the tenth edition of his *Systema Naturae* [1] Linnaeus included the 'Cat' under the scientific designation of *Felis catus*. He lived in Sweden, a country where wildcats are not found, and so he made the erroneous assumption that the domestic cat (a beast that still bears the Latin name coined by Linnaeus) was a domesticated descendant of the European animal. The type description published by Linnaeus was probably that of his own pet 'moggy'.

In 1777, the German naturalist Schreber produced a book called *A Natural History of*

-15-

- THE SMALLER MYSTERY CARNIVORES OF THE WESTCOUNTRY -

Mammals [2] in which, having had more opportunity than Linnaeus to examine the wild species, he named the European wildcat *Felis silvestris* (the forest cat). His earlier work had, incidentally, followed the nomenclature suggested by Linnaeus.

The Scottish wildcat was defined in 1907 by the British Museum; the chosen type specimen being an animal killed at Drumnadrochit on the shores of Loch Ness in 1904. Writing in *Animals and Men* during 1994 Jan Williams made the point that: [3]

> *"from this point the species 'evolved' by unnatural selection – gamekeepers supplying wildcats to museums and zoos were paid only for the ones which conformed to the type specimen".*

The accepted description of the Scottish wildcat *(F. s. grampia)* taken from *Wild Cats of the World* by C.A.W. Guggisberg (1975) [4] and *Wild Cat Species of the World* by Richard Green (1991) [5] is as follows:

The animals are larger and heavier than a domestic cat, although the size range is considerable. According to Guggisberg, 102 male Scottish wildcats were measured whose head and body measurements ranged between 36.5 cm and 65.3 cm, with a tail measurement from 21 cm to 34.2 cm.

The face and head have distinctly tabby markings, the nose is pink flesh coloured and the animals have a white throat. The ground colour of the coat is a yellowish-brown/grey and the back is far darker than the belly, which is very pale.

There is a broad, black, dorsal line made up of four or five longitudinal stripes from which a number of irregular transverse stripes run to the belly. The tail has several dark, encircling bands, of which only the last two or three count as 'rings'. The tip of the tail is black. The legs also have black bands. Green noted that the kittens are usually more strongly marked than the adults and that for the first months of their lives their tails are tapered to a point.

It is generally believed that *F. silvestris grampia* is now confined to Scotland. I have not been able to confirm whether the English specimens, which undoubtedly existed into historical times, were members of this subspecies which, by its very name, is a Scottish one. Indeed, it appears that the exact nomenclature of the English wildcat has never been decided, and I would suggest, in the light of the information in this chapter, that further research needs to be done.

There have been reports of these animals from the border counties until very recently, but it also appears that they may have survived in the Southwest of England.

According to Dr. Karl Shuker, in *Mystery Cats of the World*, [6] Devon naturalist

The most conventionally recognised depiction of the Scottish subspecies of the forest wildcat (*Felis silvestris grampia*). As has been shown in recent years, however, this commonly accepted representation may not actually be typical of the true form of the animal itself, and further research on its morphology, and the taxonomy of the wildcats of England and Wales needs to be carried out!

Trevor Beer saw some creatures that appeared to be wildcats on Exmoor in 1984. Cats which have the appearance of wildcats have been seen on Haldon Hill and at Holcombe near Dawlish.

In her book *Living on Exmoor*, which was published in 1963, Hope Bourne describes fox-sized cats which had a local reputation for ferocity which were living in the area of Room Hill immediately before the First World War. [7]

Karl Shuker wrote that: [6]

> *"Their ferocity was renowned throughout the area – apparently, not even the farm dogs would dare to attack them, and the cats would unhesitatingly kill any farm cats they encountered. Fred Milton, past president of the Exmoor Pony Society, recalled to Bourne one of his own sightings, when he observed one of these cats slinking down a nearby lane."*

Similar animals have also been reported from the Exeter area. According to a number of witnesses, here was a large and thriving population of 'wild cats', which appeared to be at least 50% larger than a normal domestic 'moggy', living wild in the St. Leonard's area of the city as recently as the late 1970s. They frequented an area of wasteland, which was, at the time, one of the few remaining legacies of Hitler's bombing campaign, although they disappeared after the area was redeveloped in the early 1980s.

On at least one occasion, kittens from this colony were adopted by local residents, and they appeared to settle into a life of cosy domesticity with relative ease. One particularly large 'tom', which was described to me as being the dominant animal of the colony, reportedly measured over 3½ feet from nose tip to tail tip. This would, by anyone's standards, have been a remarkable cat, but as we shall see, this sized animal is not unknown in the annals of the Westcountry felidae!

Such cats have usually been dismissed by most commentators as being feral domestic animals. The descriptions of the 'true' Scottish wildcat were cited to prove that whatever such animals were, they could not be *F.s.grampia*. In 1994, however, it emerged that no-one really knew what the definition of a 'true' Wildcat actually was! [8]

Jan Williams wrote that a study by Scottish Natural Heritage, at draft report stage, during the autumn of 1994, reached the conclusion that it is impossible to differentiate between *F.s.grampia* and domestic cats on the basis of markings, skull size or even genetic testing. The research was carried out at the request of the Scottish Office, following a court case in 1990 in which a gamekeeper was accused of killing three Scottish wildcats, protected under the 1981 Wildlife and Countryside Act. The case had to be dropped because no expert witness could verify that the animals were, in fact, Wildcats.

Genetic testing established distinct groups of larger cats in various parts of the Highlands. While most of the animals in these groups resemble the traditional wildcat, some have widely variable markings, including large patches of white or black. David Balharry of SNH states:

> *"There is a type of cat that the environment is selecting in some areas ... Whether that population is a remnant of the original Scottish Wildcat, I don't know."*

Planned future research included comparing the DNA from bones of ancient cats from the Inchnadamph Caves with that of modern cats. As Jan Williams pointed out, research to date left the true Scottish wildcat (if there is still such an animal) with no legal protection, and many museums displaying animals that may well be feral domestic cats.

A tabby, striped coat and bushy tail, with distinct bands are just as likely to be found on a domestic, or a feral cat.

This description certainly fits the animals seen in the Southwest in recent years. It also compares well with the description of the animals described by Hope Bourne in 1965. (The description is taken verbatim from *Mystery Cats of the World*): [9]

> *"He described it as being about the size of a male fox with a grey or tawny grey pelage marked all over with dark stripes. Its head seemed very large in comparison with that of a domestic cat, its fangs protruded below its lip, its limbs appeared to be rather long, (especially the hind pair), it walked with a slouching gait and its tail was blunt".*

I have a number of records in my files of creatures described variously as 'outsized tabbies', or as 'big grey cats'. These should not be confused with the 'big' cats reported from so much of the country in recent years. The descriptions are of animals which measure between 30 and 48 inches in length (including tail), a size which makes them larger than most feral cats which have been reported but still within the upper ranges of wildcats described by Guggisberg. [10] I tend to discount the largest animals reported, and feel that the sizes in those reports may have been exaggerated by, say, ten per cent. This would still, however, leave us with a population of sizeable cats in much of rural Devon.

Similar creatures have also been reported from Cornwall. One of our correspondents, who now lives in South Wales, has a cat that he was given when his family lived in Cornwall. He was told, by the animal's original owner, that it was descended from a 'Cornish wildcat'. This, of course, may merely have meant that the cat's antecedents were feral farmyard felines, or it may be a clue of a more cryptozoological nature. The photographs printed below certainly show that he is an impressive creature. His owner wrote to me on the 26th October 1996, enclosing the photographs and a hair sample:

> *"His vital statistics are body length 23 inches, tail length 11.5 inches, total body length 34.5 inches and weight about fifteen pounds. (Yes, you can see I am not metricated).*
>
> *When we lived close to the sea in Cornwall, he would often come home with seabirds he had caught and now hardly a day goes by without a 'present' from him of a vole, shrew, mouse or bird on the front doorstep! Another one of his tricks was to be on a rock surrounded by water, we never worked out how he did it as he never appeared to be wet. Yet, in spite of all this he is one of the most peaceable cats ever, he often allows himself to be bullied by cats a fraction of his size and yet he is not very affectionate. Another of his claims to fame is that he survived both barrels of a shotgun at close range and being left to die. On both occasions he dragged himself back home and on both occasions the vet wanted to put him out of his misery, hence he is probably the most expensive cat alive!"*

My correspondent went on to note that this remarkable cat also catches rabbits. At the time of writing, there has not been any result from the analysis of the hair samples, although both Mitochondrial DNA and Electron Microscopy tests are planned. The photographs are also, unfortunately, inconclusive, and do not show an animal which conforms to the traditional wildcat descriptions. Nevertheless, as we have seen, the traditional view of wildcat morphology is open to a certain amount of re-interpretation.

There is no doubt that there are some extraordinarily large farm cats in Cornwall. We were one of the first investigators at Ninestones Farm on Bodmin Moor. There had been reports of 'panther' and 'lynx' like animals, but some of the farm cats owned by Mrs. Rhodes, the farmer, were extraordinarily large. One in particular, 'Thomas', was probably the largest domestic cat I have ever seen. Indeed, it seems probable that, in the light of the findings of the MAFF report of 1995, 'Thomas' was responsible for at least one of the video clips purporting to be of 'The Beast of Bodmin'.

These animals have also been seen in more rural areas. During an investigation that the Centre for Fortean Zoology carried out into a series of 'big cat' sightings in the Kingsteignton and Newton Abbot areas, [11] one witness, 'Andrew G', spoke of a large grey 'tabby' he had seen in Forde Park.

'Andrew G' had spent something in the region of half an hour watching this animal 'stalking its prey' in scrubland on the edges of the park. Other reports of these large tabby cats from the area imply that these creatures are well established in the park. One verbal description of what appears to be one of the large grey animals is extremely interesting because the witness noted that the tail of the creature was particularly tapered. For a possible explanation of this animal, we must go across the sea to Ireland, where a minor cryptozoological mystery has been puzzling researchers for over a hundred years.

Although it is a common figure in Celtic-Hibernian folklore, the wildcat has never officially been recorded from the island of Ireland. There have, however, been isolated records of what appear to be genuine Irish wildcats for centuries.

One specimen, described by the famous 19th Century naturalist, the Rev. J.G. Wood, seems very similar to the animals reported from Newton Abbott:

> *"..of a dirty grey colour, double the size of a common house cat, and its teeth and claws more than proportionally larger."* [12][13]

In 1904, a series of sub-fossil remains were found in two caves in County Clare. When he described them to the British Association, [14] Dr. R.F. Scharff found that, much to his surprise, the remains seemed to be comparable with the African wildcat (*F.lybica*) rather than of the European species. He compared jaws and teeth from specimens found in Egyptian tombs with the Irish bones, and with contemporary bones, to reach his conclusion. (See Appendix One). This is particularly interesting for two reasons. Firstly, it is now generally agreed that *F.catus* is basically a domesticated descendant of *F.lybica* rather than the European species, and secondly, one of the distinguishing characteristics of *F.lybica* is its tapering tail. I have pointed out elsewhere in this chapter, although it is generally assumed that the wildcat population, which was found in Southern England into historic times, was of the same creature currently found in Scotland. This however, has never been proved, and in zoology, as in life, it is never safe to make assumptions without the facts to back them up.

Even more interesting are animals which have been reported to me as 'outsized Siamese cats'. These animals have been most usually reported from the Newton Abbot and Teignbridge areas, but have been seen as far away as Powderham and Dartington. It is interesting how homogenous the reports of the outsized 'Siamese' type cats are. They mention the long limbs and slouching gait of the Exmoor creatures described by Hope Bourne, but also mention a black mask like a pure bred Siamese cat. These 'super-Siamese' animals appear to hunt, often in pairs, at dawn and dusk. One witness saw a pair near Kenton and a few weeks later, a single individual on the road between Ipplepen and Newton Abbot. [15] He described an animal of about 36 inches in length (from nose tip to tail tip) and he said that friends of his had seen the same (or a very similar animal).

'Andrew G.', described a series of attacks on domestic poultry in suburban Kingsteignton. [16] I have received other reports of attacks on domestic fowl from the area and it seems not coincidental that so many of these attacks have taken place in the region

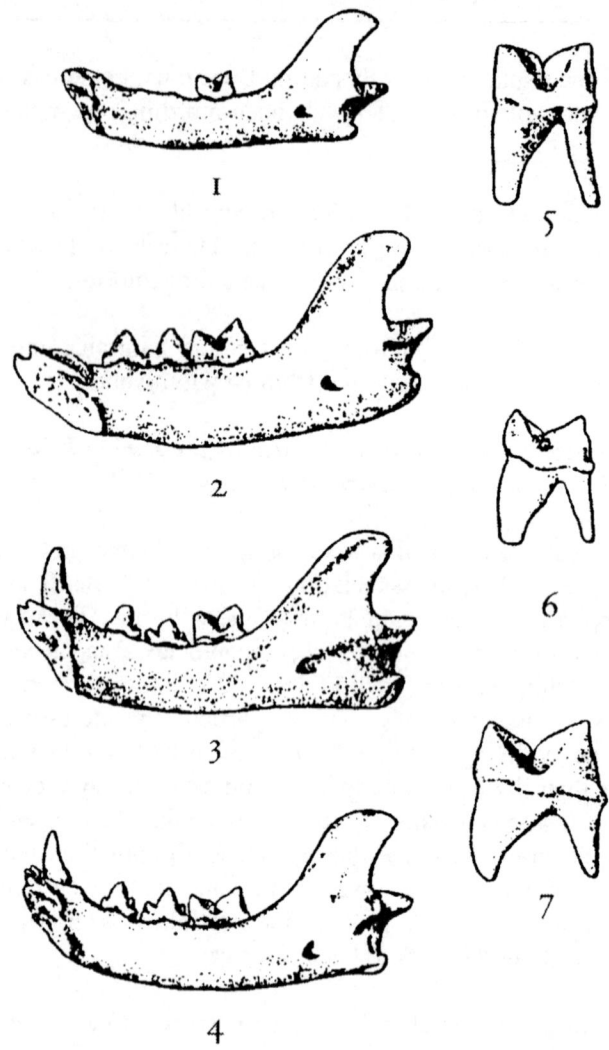

Comparison of jaw-bones found in Newhall Caves, Ireland with those taken from other cats – after R.F.Scharfe (1906).

1. Right ramus of the lower jaw of dwarf form of domestic cat *(F.catus)* from Newhall caves.
2. Right ramus of the lower jaw of African wildcat *(F.lybica)* from Newhall caves.
3. Right ramus of the lower jaw of European wildcat *(F.silvestris)* from Inverness, Scotland.
4. Right ramus of the lower jaw of African mummy cat *(F.lybica)* from Egyptian tomb.
5. Lower carnassial tooth of European wildcat *(F.silvestris)* from Inverness, Scotland.
6. Lower carnassial tooth of domestic cat *(F.catus)* from Cappagh, Co. Waterford.
7. Lower carnassial tooth of African wildcat *(F.lybica)* from Newhall Caves.

NOTE: *The roots of the teeth in figs. 6 and 7 should be twisted more to the right in order to give an exact idea of their position in the alveoli.*

where so many of these large feral cats of various types have been seen.

It is interesting to note that when pure bred Siamese cats interbreed with other races of *F. catus* (or, presumably, other cat species); the distinctive colouration is usually lost. The offspring of such mating are usually black or tabby, although the 'kink' in the tail and the pointed face can be inherited. There have been no reports of animals with 'kinky' tails living wild in mid-Devon. The reports of sizeable creatures with 'Siamese' markings and features continue and I feel that it is unlikely that all the animals reported could be stray 'pure bred' Siamese cats. It is even more unlikely that hypothetical colonies of 'stray' Siamese would breed true, and so these animals, whatever they are, are a real mystery.

The 'super-Siamese' cats, the large grey striped cats, and the 'outsized tabbies', which have also been seen in other parts of the Southwestern peninsula would, prior to 1994, be dismissed as 'feral' cats. The SNH findings would suggest that perhaps this may not be so.

Various animal welfare charities have made suggestions as to the numbers of feral cats living wild in the British Isles. Numbers of up to seven figures have been mooted. [17] What seems almost certain is that the genetic stock of any but the most remote colonies of *F.s.grampia* will have been diluted by the addition of genes from *F.catus*.

The genetic identity of whatever cats are living wild in the British countryside (they should probably not be referred to as 'Wildcats' anymore), would seem to have become even more complicated in recent years.

Zoologist Dr. Ingvald Lieberkind, in his Danish Encyclopaedia *Dyrenes Verden* from the mid-sixties, noted that the domestic cat has, on occasion, hybridised with the following species: [18][19]

- *Felis chaus*
- *F. Silvestris*
- *F.s. ocreata*
- *F.s. ornata*
- *F.s. cafra*
- *F. lynx*

It is also accepted that *F. catus* can hybridise with other species including the Bengal leopard cat (*P.bengalensis*). [20] Four of the cats in Dr. Lieberkind's list are the forest wildcat and three of its sub-species, but the other animals are larger and more exotic animals.

A brief description of each species will suffice, but it is interesting to note that, in two out of the three species, introduced specimens have been killed in the British Isles.

In the third species, there is a body of contemporary folklore to suggest that its presence in the area might not be particularly unlikely.

The Jungle Cat (*Felis chaus*)

Guggisberg describes a creature 'larger than the forest wildcat' with 'long legs, a comparatively short tail, and small pencils of black hair on its ears'. The average head and body length is 24 inches (60 cms), with a further 9 inches of tail. The animal stands about 14 inches at the shoulders. The colouration ranges from sandy to reddish brown.

They are found all over the Middle East and southern Asia, [21] and were well known to the ancient Egyptians who, according to some accounts, trained them as semi-domesticated hunting animals. Although, according to some accounts in the literature on British Alien Big Cats, they are an uncommon animal in captivity, according to several of my informants within the world of animal husbandry, they are quite regularly kept in collections. Certainly, the Dartmoor Wildlife Park had them in 1995, and a paper by Simon Baker of MAFF, [22] listing escaped exotic animals, made mention of several captive specimens kept under license.

Richard Green lists nine sub-species, and notes that up to seven kittens can be born in each litter. I have no records of which sub-species have been kept in captivity in British zoos, but what is certain is, that on at least three occasions (listed by Baker), animals of this species have escaped and lived wild, for a time at least, in the English countryside. [23]

One was killed by a car on Hayling Island in Hampshire during the summer of 1988. This was apparently part of a pair which had been seen on the island for some time. Another, whose preserved body is now in the collection of Dr. Shuker, was discovered dead in Shropshire in February 1989. [24]

Dr. Shuker wrote a couple of articles for *Fortean Times* [25][26] about the existence of *F. chaus* x *F.catus* hybrids in the West Midlands, and illustrated the second with a photograph of a cat called 'Jasper', the pet of a lady in Leintwardine in Shropshire. He discussed the evidence, which suggested that especially as the Shropshire Jungle Cat had been living wild for up to five years; many of the medium-sized mystery cats seen in the area were probably his descendants. He also suggested that 'Jasper' was probably a second generation hybrid descendant.

Dr. Shuker collated a number of reports of this species from the West Midlands, and it appears that, as in their native India, these animals, or at least their hybrids, are filling a similar ecological niche to that usually filled in the UK by the Urban Fox.

Jungle Cat killed in Shropshire 1988

Picture courtesy of Dr. Karl Shuker

'Jasper'

Picture courtesy of Dr. Karl Shuker

The final word on *Felis chaus* must come from Karl Shuker, who told me, late one night on the telephone, that although he had read the descriptions of the Shropshire jungle cat, and of the species as a whole, that it was not until he actually had the animal in a glass case in front of him that he realised quite what an impressive animal it was!

The Lynx (*Felis lynx*)

The lynx is a solitary, medium-sized cat with fairly long fur which grows longer in winter. It is 80-130 cm in length with an extra 11 to 24.5 cm of tail. Standing up to 75 cm at the shoulder and weighing up to 35 kg, it is quite a formidable beast. [27][28] It has a yellowish-brown coat marked with more or less distinct dark spots. The colour of the spots varies according to the geographical location. The lynx has long sturdy legs, a very short tail, and triangular ears topped by tufts of black hairs about 4 cm in length. Both sexes carry well-developed side whiskers which, during winter, can take on almost mane-like proportions.

Although it is currently agreed that Linnaeus' original Latin nomenclature is correct, for many years the lynx was considered to belong to a separate genus, 'Lynx', which also included the North American bobcat. Guggisberg considered that the Spanish or Isabelline lynx was merely a regional variant of the main species, although he listed the bobcat as distinct at a specific level.

Richard Green, however, lists the lynx, the Spanish lynx (*Felis pardina*) and the bobcat (*Felis rufus*) as separate species, although he admits that some authorities still refer to *F. pardina* as being distinct only at sub-specific level. He lists nine sub-species of *F. lynx*, twelve of *F. rufus* and only one sub-species of *F. pardina*.

To confuse the matter further, the African caracal is also often referred to as a 'lynx'.

There have been a number of reports of 'caracals' from Cornwall over the past thirty years, and whereas, to my knowledge, the only Cornish caracals are a pair owned by my friend and colleague Chris Moiser, which reside at Porfell Country Wildlife Park, the reports should not, as we shall see, be dismissed out of hand.

As noted elsewhere in this book, my ex-wife and I were amongst the first investigators to visit Ninestones Farm on Bodmin Moor at the height of the first spate of 'Beast of Bodmin' reports. Indeed, although I cannot actually prove it, it was I who coined the term 'Beast of Bodmin' and sincerely recommended to Mrs. Rhodes, the farmer whose livestock was being decimated, that she copyright the name! If she had done so she would, by now, be a very wealthy woman! She showed me a watercolour painting that had been given to her of an animal seen in the vicinity by the artist. This picture, which has been shown on television on at least one occasion, was of an animal that very much resembled a caracal. Similar animals have been reported from other parts of Cornwall,

- THE SMALLER MYSTERY CARNIVORES OF THE WESTCOUNTRY -

Canada Lynx (*Lynx canadensis*)

Are animals of this, or a closely related species, roaming the wilder parts of the United Kingdom?

including Ponsanooth, just outside Falmouth!

But is there any historically valid basis for these sightings, and if these animals DO exist, how long have they been here?

There have been reports of mystery 'big cats' from different parts of Britain for centuries, and so many records of lynx-like creatures have been catalogued that Bernard Heuvelmans, the 'father' of cryptozoology, [30] and the noted Devon naturalist H.G. Hurrell, [31] (who we will meet again in a later chapter) have both suggested, quite seriously, that this species may still exist in Britain. It should, I feel, be mentioned here, that when I contacted Hurrell's daughter, she categorically denied that her father had made any such assertions. Miss Hurrell, as will become clear later in this book, disapproves of it and wishes to have nothing to do with us or this project.

It is interesting to note, however, that reports of lynx-like animals in Britain are not a modern phenomenon. The 16th Century author, Ralph Holinshead wrote:

> "Lions we have had very many in the north parts of Scotland and those with manes of no less force than those of Mauritania; but how and when

they were destroyed I do not yet read".

It has been suggested, by various authors, that this is valuable evidence for the one-time existence of an indigenous species of British big cat. I feel that this is highly unlikely, but the report undoubtedly exists. [41]

Another, often quoted, report is from William Cobbett's *Rural Rides*, published in 1830. [43] As a boy he had spotted a cat the size of a 'middle-sized spaniel dog' which went up into a hollow elm tree. When he returned home, he was scolded for telling untruths, but as he wrote:

> "I have since many times repeated it and I would take my oath of it to this day. When in New Brunswick I saw the great wild grey cat, which is there called a Lucifee, and it seemed to me to be just such a cat as I had seen at Waverley".

In view of the rest of his writings, Cobbett's testimony can be wholeheartedly trusted. He was a remarkable man! Nearly a century and a half later, another great English writer, the late Sir John Verney, a man who I had the privilege of corresponding with during his last few years, described Cobbett: [44]

> "A giant of a man - in every sense ... Farmer, writer, political commentator"

His *Rural Rides*, which continued the account of what appears to be an 18th Century British lynx sighting, were perhaps his greatest achievement. In 1973, Verney wrote:

> "In the 1820s when he was over sixty, he rode around England recording what he found in robust, hard hitting prose. He detested the changes coming over the country – the early stages of the Industrial Revolution. The same thing that Blake meant by 'Dark Satanic Mills' – although they were nothing to what followed ..."

As well as being a writer, Cobbett was active in politics and social reform. As Verney explained, he was even a Member of Parliament:

> "... right at the end of his life, after he'd done more than anyone to bring about the First Reform Bill. He was one of the founders of contemporary democracy but I doubt whether he'd have approved of it. And I'm sure he wouldn't have fitted into any of the present political parties. Perhaps he'd have concerned himself more with things like pollution and conservation"...

From this, and from other accounts of his life, it is clear that Cobbett was a remarkable man, and that his testimony is not to be dismissed lightly. It is not as if his are the only records of lynx-like animals from the British Isles prior to the 1975 Dangerous Wild Animals Act, which, it is theorised was directly responsible for the release of so many new animals into the ecosystem of the British Isles. Di Francis writes: [41]

> *"The Daily Express reported on the 14th January 1927 that, following a number of livestock being killed and strange footprints being discovered, a farmer killed a 'large, fierce yellow animal of unknown species'. However, the slaughter continued. Another animal similar to the first was shot, then a third was trapped. 'The body was sent to the London Zoo where it was identified as that of a lynx'. However, London Zoo has no record in its files of receiving the animal, and one wonders, anyway, just what was sent in for identification. The creature was shot in Inverness-shire and without freezing the body would be in a rather advanced state of decomposition on arrival. If it was just the skin that was dispatched to London, a true identification was unlikely".*

The problem which occurs again and again when dealing with oft quoted archival reports like this one is that, although the 'records' of Inverness lynxes are now firmly entrenched in the fortean archives and perforce in the collective consciousness of those who study such things, the solid evidence for these incidents is negligible.

We have one oft repeated newspaper report, by a journalist who, as at the time of writing, first published the report nearly seventy years ago, is almost certainly dead, and who may well have made it all up anyway. Equally well, he may not have done, but unlike the testimony of Cobbett, which, as we have seen, seems, on the surface at least, to be above reproach, we feel that the 1927 report should be treated *cum grano salis*!

Whilst it is quite certain that lynx, together with scimitar cats and the cave leopard were once a well-known feature of the British ecosystem, it is generally accepted that they died out with the last Ice-Age, and I feel that it is highly unlikely that any of these species have survived unscathed to the present day.

'Highly unlikely' is not, however, synonymous with 'impossible'!

What is more likely, however, is that they were introduced into the area in far more recent historical times. One of the strangest things about crypto-investigative theory is that the folklore surrounding it occurs over and over again in different parts of the world.

Bernie Mace, of the New South Wales Rare Fauna Research Group in Australia told me in 1990 that one of the recurrent pieces of folklore used to explain the occurrence of 'mystery' cats in Australia, was that they were the descendants of animals liberated by U.S. soldiers during the war. According to widespread antipodean belief, several regiments of American soldiers stationed in Australia had bobcats and pumas as mas-

The lynx as depicted in
Edward Topsell's *History of Four-footed Beasts*, 1607

cots and that when the regiments were posted to a war-zone, the animals were liberated rather than be destroyed.

It is an incontrovertible fact that Southwestern England was host to a number of transatlantic regiments during the Second World War. The 'dry runs' for the D-Day landings took place at Slapton in the South Hams, and on Braunton Burrows, and I suppose that it is not surprising that, I have been told in confidence, but in all seriousness, the same story that Bernie Mace was told in Australia. To me, this scenario seems highly unlikely, but lynx-like cats have been reported on a regular basis, in Devon and Cornwall, as well as elsewhere in the country over the last fifty years.

The story of the wartime mascots has proved almost impossible to substantiate. Acting on the advice of my father, who has unerringly steered me in the right direction in matters like this, I wrote to the Military Attaché at the United States Embassy in London and also to the office of the Canadian High Commissioner. In both letters, I requested details of wartime postings in the Southwest, and in each case I drew a blank. Eight months later, after repeated attempts, I had heard nothing at all from the Canadians, while the Americans merely wrote to me with a photocopied list of Anglo-US friendship associations, aimed at the families of 'GI Brides', and despite further attempts at seeking the truth I heard nothing more of the matter.

In Australia, however, it has been a different matter. A recent book on *Australian Mystery Beasts* by Healey and Cropper (1994), has gone much further than I have in providing corroborative evidence for this undeniably attractive piece of folklore. [45]

"Some of the most interesting evidence uncovered by the Deakin University team in 1976/7 was found not in the field but in the archives. While attempting to nail down the regimental mascot theory, they eventually discovered the identity of two American units which were stationed around Mt. Gambier in 1942. They were the 35th and 46th Pursuit (Fighter) Groups. The units later moved to Queensland and then to the Pacific Islands.

Digging deeper the researchers hit what appeared to be the jackpot: they found that the colour flash emblems of both groups displayed the outline of large black cats!"

It seems quite likely from this, and from other evidence presented by Healey and Cropper, that the Australian myth at least has some truth behind it. Maybe a future researcher will be able to prove the same thing about its British counterpart. As someone or other once said: "The Truth is Out There"! [see footnote]

Bengal Leopard Cat (*Prionailurus bengalensis*)

According to Guggisberg, "the leopard cat is about the size of a domestic cat although it stands higher". [32] Although the species was first described from India in 1792, it is found all across Southern Asia, from Manchuria to Sumatra, and several animals, originally described as separate species are know considered to belong to *P. bengalensis*. Richard Green lists ten distinct sub-species. [33]

The zoologist, C.H. Keeling, told me that the type specimen was caught swimming far from land in the Bay of Bengal, and books on the wildlife of Hong Kong, where, since the leopard and the tiger no longer exist there, it is the only indigenous felid, note it as a strong swimmer. [34]

In recent years, they have been kept as 'exotic' pets in the UK, and although they are a proscribed species under the terms of the 1977 Dangerous Wild Animals Act, they continue to be kept. A number of these delightful little animals have been shot in recent years across the country. One pair, being kept illegally by a drug dealer and petty criminal on Dartmoor, were accidentally liberated in 1987 when the Police and the Ministry of Agriculture raided his house. Although the male was shot some months later near Widecombe-in-the-Moor, the female was never caught. [35] [36] [37]

---

1. I should really have known better. This was the phrase included in every episode of the popular television programme *The X-Files*. The series came to an end some years ago, and as I hope that this book will have a considerable shelf life, it will probably be around long after the exploits of Messrs Scully and Mulder are forgotten. That is the problem with including contemporary references in ones writings.

I had a similar problem when considering the music I wrote in the 1980s for reissue. Several of my best loved songs were rants about then premier Thatcher, and other issues which are now completely obsolete. Such is life!

There are several other records of this species from the southern part of Britain. I was surprised to find out that it was so widely kept, but it appears that there is even a relatively new breed of 'domestic cat' called 'the Bengal', (originally the 'ozicat') after a supposed resemblance to an ocelot, which was obtained by hybridising *P.bengalensis* with *F.catus* and then 'back crossing' the hybrids with *F.catus* in order to produce a domestic cat which retained the leopard cat colouration. [38]

We have at least three interesting and exotic potential variants to the gene pool of feral cattery in Devonshire. The addition of the genes of each of these species has exciting and frightening implications for both the ecologist and the taxonomist. We have already seen how the genetic identity of the native forest wildcat has been cast severely into doubt. The entry of these new and relatively little studied chromosomal additions to the genetic pool seems likely to give rise to some bizarre and unlikely animals.

The anatomy and physiology of one series of complex introgressive hybrids between *F.catus* and *F.Silvestris grampia*, led in the mid-1980s to the discovery of what many people, for a while at least, considered to be a new and distinct species of British felid; the Kellas cat. [39]

During the mid-1980s, a series of mysterious creatures, the size of a traditional wildcat, but with coarse black hair sprinkled with white primary guard hairs, were killed in Western Scotland. These creatures were mostly found in the vicinity of the West Moray hamlet of Kellas. Their behaviour was markedly different from Scottish wildcats. They hunted in pairs, and unlike *F.s.grampia* they did not appear to be arboreal. [40]

They were unusually gracile and presented other characteristics which suggested they might be a new species, or at the very least a species in the process of emerging. Eventually, the hypothesis proposed by Dr. Karl Shuker in *Mystery Cats of the World* (1989) was proved correct. The animals proved to be a complex introgressive hybrid between *F.s.grampia* and *F.catus*. The precise nature of the hybridisation is, however, presently unclear.

If a complex introgressive hybrid between two such well-known species can create such taxonomic confusion, I will end this chapter by asking the reader to consider what a variety of peculiar cats, of all shapes and sizes, could be produced by the introgressive hybridisation of some, or all, of the species mentioned in this chapter.

I have tried to avoid mention of the British Alien Big Cats in this chapter. Their existence is not in doubt, but their identity, at least at the time of writing, remains a complete mystery. It seems likely that pumas, at least, are also living wild in the British countryside. The size difference between the lynx and the puma is not considerable, and so it is not inconceivable that *P.concolor* has also added its distinctive genetic pat-

THE SMALLER MYSTERY CARNIVORES OF THE WESTCOUNTRY

terns to the common gene pool.

There is also one final possibility. This is that the occurrence of 'outsized' cats in the British countryside is not a new phenomenon at all. Throughout this chapter we have discussed the various theories hinging on the introduction of exotic species into the gene pool of the feral cat/wildcat population. For centuries, there have been isolated reports of medium-sized, and even larger, feline predators at large across Britain. Whilst I find it hard to accept theories like those of Mrs. Di Francis, that the British 'big cat' is a surviving, though evolved, descendant of one or more species of antediluvian big cat, including sabre-toothed tigers, [41] it is hard not to ignore that anecdotal evidence for smaller predators. In issue 17 of the excellent zoological publication *Mainly about Animals*, [42] Peter Sharp noted that, even in the 1920s, rabbit trappers would occasionally catch 'very large' cats in their snares. He theorised that there is some genetic mechanism within the feral cat population that occasionally produces very large specimens. Certainly many of the hair samples allegedly from 'mystery cats' appear to be very similar to those obtained from *F.catus*. In the past, this has been used as supporting evidence to disprove the existence of mystery 'big' cats in the UK.

Perhaps it is nothing of the kind!

Mounted Specimen of Kellas Cat

Pictures courtesy of Benjiman McDhui CFZ

- CHAPTER TWO -
THE POLECAT

'A skunk is better company than someone who prides himself on being frank!'

Lazarus Long

The polecat, *Mustela putorius* is an animal that has had a long historical relationship with mankind. Men have kept polecats, usually in their domesticated and albino/partially albino phase, as 'ferrets' for thousands of years, and the exact taxonomic position of the ferret within the taxonomy of the mustelidae as a whole is unclear.

This description of the species is paraphrased from *A Guide to the Mammals of Britain and Europe* by Maurice Burton (1976). [1] This will begin to prove exactly HOW much confusion there is surrounding this creature. According to Burton, it has long, coarse fur which is very dark brown on the upper parts of the body with dense, yellowish under-fur showing through. The under parts are black. There are white or yellow patches between the ears and eyes and on the muzzle. The ears are small; it has short legs and a black, bushy tail.

The long cylindrical body is slung low and has a long neck. The anal glands have an unpleasant smelling secretion. Burton admits that there is a considerable variation in colour, with paler and redder forms well-known. The female is slightly smaller than the male and only a little over half the weight. The male has an average head and body length of about 410 mm (16 in), with an extra 180 mm (7 in) or so of tail, and will weigh up to 2.05 kg (4.5 lb).

The creature is found throughout Europe as far north as southern Sweden and even southern Finland. It lives in thickets, woods and scrubland, sometimes surprisingly close to human habitation. A documentary shown on television in 1992 or 1993 showed a female (Jill) polecat bring up a family of babies in a semi-disused barn on a Welsh mountain farm. They mate in March or April and have a gestation period of about six weeks. They probably only produce one litter a year in the wild, with three to eight (usually five or six) young. The babies (kits) are born blind and pure white, with the distinctive adult markings not usually appearing until about the age of three months. The kits remain with the Jill until the autumn. The male (Hob) takes no part in the rearing of the litter.

The main food source for polecats is rats, mice and rabbits, although other small animals, birds, amphibians and reptiles are also taken. They hunt with the aid of a highly developed sense of smell. The predations on both domestic poultry and game from this creature cannot be denied, although it does appear that some of the lurid descriptions of its prowess as a killer of chickens may have been somewhat exaggerated.

The animals are solitary, terrestrial and nocturnal. They move with a peculiar gliding action which Burton describes as being "more like swimming than running", but which has always reminded me, irresistibly of a small, furry snake. They build their den in any convenient hole such as a fox earth or rock crevice. The breeding nests are always made of dry grass or hay.

The Polecat as depicted in
Edward Topsell's *History of Four-footed Beasts*, 1607

The Polecat *(Mustela putorious)*

Burton notes that, although they are usually silent they sometimes yelp, cluck or chatter. I have noted that solitary males in captivity also sometimes make a curious barking sound, which sounds very similar to that made by a male muntjac or barking deer. The peculiar thing about this odd 'coughing' bark is that the male will do it every night for about a week and then will be silent for several months. There does not seem to be any correlation between these sounds and the breeding cycle. I have never noticed it when a female in the next cage is in oestrus, or when the animal has a companion of either sex in his cage. These episodes of barking usually happen every two or three months, and more often in the winter. There does not seem to be any correlation between these sounds and the phases of the moon.

Ferrets are sometimes treated as a distinct species *Putorius puro*. It is uncertain whether the ferret bloodline is purely a domesticated variety of the Eurasian polecat, which is what, on the surface it appears to be, or whether it is actually a domesticated descendent of a complex series of hybridisations between the Eurasian polecat and other closely allied species, like the steppe polecat, which is superficially very similar to the Eurasian species, but is found further east, or the marbled polecat (*Vormela peregusna*), an attractive little creature found in Eastern Europe. There is also every chance that North American ferrets may have some genetic inheritance from the native, and exceedingly rare, black footed ferret.

There is no doubt, whatsoever, that ferrets are kept widely throughout the country, and especially in the Southwest. This is a semi rural population with below the national average income, a higher than average unemployment rate, and a large rabbit population. This means that the creatures are kept, rather than is the norm these days as mildly exotic pets (we have a number of them for precisely this reason), but as aids for the hunter or poacher.

It is also beyond doubt that large numbers of these creatures escape every year and have established themselves locally in feral populations. The important thing to try and ascertain, is whether any of the original polecat population (which was supposedly wiped out over eighty years ago) is still extant, and whether the introduced ferrets have:

a.   Bolstered up the gene pool of a flagging population.
b.   Filled the ecological niche left by a vanished population.
                              or
c.   Wiped out the remaining polecat population and replaced them.

In historical times, the polecat was common in the region. Writing in a paper for the Devonshire Association, Brushfield (1897) searched the rural parish records in search of mentions of this and other species destroyed as vermin: [2]

> *"Polecat: The destruction of this animal is recorded in the majority of annals of rural parishes and it is entered under various names; 'Fichew', 'Polcat', and 'Fulmer', or 'Foumart'; 'Polecat' being probably the least frequent.*
>
> *Chaucer has 'Polcat' and Topsell 'Poul Cat'. This, one writer affirms to be a corruption of 'Poulcat', poultry having been especially subject to its attacks, but Professor Skeat has shown this to be incorrect.*
>
> *In the southern parts of England, it is generally known as 'Fitch' or one of its numerous variants. In payments noted in the Hartland warden's accounts of the 17th Century, 'Feetches' and 'Fitchewes' and 'Fitch' are the terms employed.*
>
> *Although the Weasel tribe, generally, is notorious for its destruction of*

poultry and game (...) by far the worst offender is the Polecat. It is the most determined enemy of all game preserves, poultry yards, and rabbit warrens, but whereas all the other animals that prey upon the same birds kill what they need, eating it on the spot or carrying it to their den, this one appears to destroy for the sheer pleasure of killing, plundering and destroying all within reach. (...) It is said to be diminishing in its numbers in Britain, and the traps of the gamekeeper and the gun of the farmer are probably the main cause. It will catch fish, or live off rats, mice and small vermin, like the stoat or the marten, but not to the same extent that they do.

Taking all this into consideration, the wonder is not that the animal was killed at the expense of the parish, but that the payments for its destruction are not more frequent. None are recorded in the annals of Woodbury and Littleham. In East Budleigh, twenty were paid for between the year 1668 and 1679, but no others were noticed in the warden's accounts. (...) In 1824, great slaughter was committed amongst the Foumarts, twenty two seniors and five juniors being duly presented and paid for".

It is interesting to note that in a recent (1987) book on *Pet Ferrets*, [3] published for the American market, the strain of ferret with the 'wild' polecat markings, which appears to be bred for pet keeping and docility rather than for its hunting ability, is still known as a 'fitch ferret'.

According to accepted belief, although the polecat was known in the wild from all parts of mainland Britain during historical times, by the early part of the 20th Century they were confined to parts of Scotland and Wales. This is another fallacy and, again, is one that Langley and Yalden have been instrumental in perpetuating. [4]

What is certain is that the Westcountry records of these creatures did not end when Langley and Yalden said that they did. I would like to present a brief summary of the 20th Century records of the polecat in the four counties we have cited from Langley and Yalden's paper.

SOMERSET

There are three Somerset records from the earliest part of this century, the most recent being in 1919, [5] nine years after Langley and Yalden consigned them to an ignominious extinction.

DEVONSHIRE

Writing in 1953, for that year's mammal report for the Devonshire Association, the renowned Devon naturalist, H.G. Hurrell, noted that:

"No news has reached me of any recent occurrences in Devon. Major Calmady Hamlyn tells me that he knew an aged friend who formerly kept a pack of otter hounds which sometimes hunted polecats in birch wood on the banks of the Tavy. They used to baffle the hounds by running along the top of the furze bushes. The date was probably about one hundred years ago". [6]

Polecats were also hunted on Dartmoor. Writing in 1897, W.F. Collier [7] stated that there might be a few polecats left on the moor, but:

"to find one and run him down has been considered hopeless for many years".

However, in the earlier part of the 19th Century he had hunted them on Dartmoor as a 'summer sport'. Together with two or three friends:

"we used to take a few hounds to The Saracen's Head at Two Bridges to hunt the Fulmaret. This was the best sport of all".

Two were caught at Ugborough in Devon in 1918, [8] and H.G. Hurrell recorded the species from the Modbury area near Kingsbridge in 1925. [9] Two were trapped at Hatch in the South Hams in 1925. [10] Hurrell also noted another pair that was killed in the same area ten years later. [11] He also noted a Polecat seen by his cousin crossing the River Dart in 1910. [12]

There are a number of North Devon records from the first part of the century. One was killed in a cornfield in September 1937, [13] and there was a specimen killed in Combe Martin in 1906. [14] Hurrell, who obviously didn't know about the 1937 record, said that the 1935 records from Modbury were quite possibly the last English records [15] as, by the time he was writing in 1968, the British populations of the animal was confined to Wales and Scotland.

There is another record from 1930 of four creatures 'larger than stoats', which were seen playing amongst boulders at Bellever, [16] but even this record by St. Leger-Gordon and Harvey from their 1953 book 'Dartmoor' concludes with the assertion that the species is "probably extinct in the region". Even so, we have acceptable records of fifty years longer than is conceded by Langley and Yalden. [17]

There have been other records since 1937. Over the past few years considerable numbers of animals, which appear to be polecats, have been killed by traffic, especially on the M5 between Cullompton and Exeter, and on the A30 between Exeter and Okehampton. My ex-wife saw an animal that she thought was 'probably a polecat' at

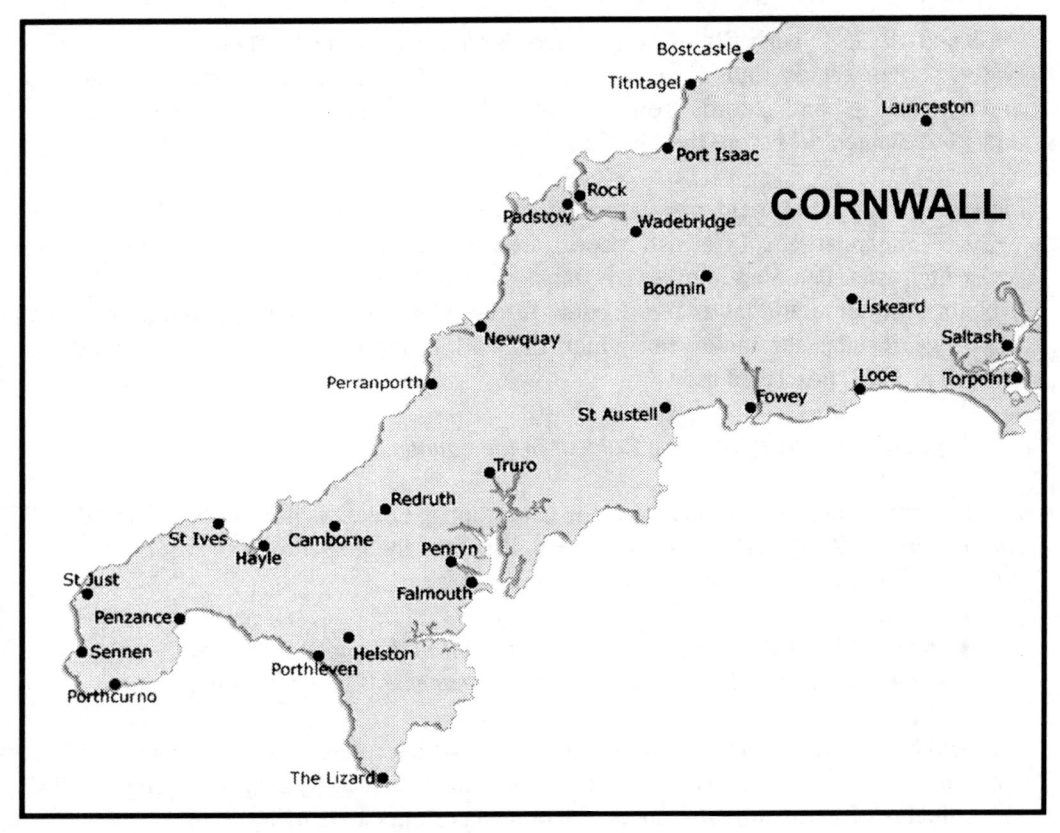

- THE SMALLER MYSTERY CARNIVORES OF THE WESTCOUNTRY -

A map of Cornwall showing places named in the text

Matford Roundabout, on the outskirts of Exeter one night in January 1995. It was hunting in some bushes, and she followed it, hoping either for a firm identification, or even to capture the animal, but it proved too elusive even for her. Unfortunately, for those who would point to these post-1937 records as firm evidence for the survival of the species in Devonshire, there are, as we shall see, many reasons to doubt the veracity of these records as far as firm evidence is concerned.

CORNWALL

The animal was found in Cornwall well within living memory. Writing in 1979, Rennie Bere said:

> *"The polecat is known to have been present in the Budock Valley near Falmouth up to 1914".* [18]

The Institute for Cornish Studies has a number of records, including two from Penryn in

1908 and 1919, [19] early 20th Century records from Boscastle, [20] Tintagel, [21] Chacewater, [22] and Lands End, [23] as well as late 19th Century records from Liskeard [24] and St. Ives, [25] and records from the valley below Budock School near Penryn, [26] and from Sennen [27] before the First World War.

Despite Langley and Yalden's statement that the animal was extinct in Cornwall by 1890, [28] the most recent Cornish records are from Goonhaven in 1934, [29] and an animal which was seen on a number of occasions near Camborne in 1942, [30] which was probably the same animal as the 'Coarse furred, black bellied ferret', found drowned near Gwealevallen the same year, which Dr. Turk of the Institute for Cornish Studies, writing in 1959, described as:

> *'possibly the last surviving Polecat in the country'.* [31]

An intriguing reference comes from Sir Christopher Lever, writing in his *Naturalised Animals of the British Isles* (1975). [32] He discusses the polecat-ferret at some length, but also mentions the 'parent' species, describing it as:

> "*probably our rarest carnivore, being confined almost exclusively to the woods and hills of Wales and parts of the extreme West of England*".

It would be particularly interesting to find out to which references Lever was referring when he mentions the 'Extreme West of England' because, by this time, even by the most liberal of estimates, the species would have appeared to have been extinct in Cornwall for something in the region of forty years!

Writing about the status of the polecat in Cornwall in 1969, Rennie Bere [53] said that the county was home to large numbers of cross-bred polecat-ferrets. (The term, unfortunately, can also be used to describe ferrets which have the colouration of wild polecats, so Bere's precise meaning is unclear).

This scenario is used repeatedly to explain sightings of wild-looking animals in areas where the wild animal is no longer found. One wonders, however, from where the wild population, that the escaped domestic animals are supposed to have interbred with, came from, when the animal, by 1969 when Bere was writing, had supposedly been extinct for nearly eighty years.

This excuse, therefore, is the least effective way of proving that a wild population no longer exists that I have ever heard. A more likely theory, but one which still smacks a little of desperation and an ineffectual attempt at making the facts fit the theories, is genetic and can be used to explain the Westcountry sightings of both polecats and wildcats.

When the domesticated creatures were first liberated, they then, theoretically at least,

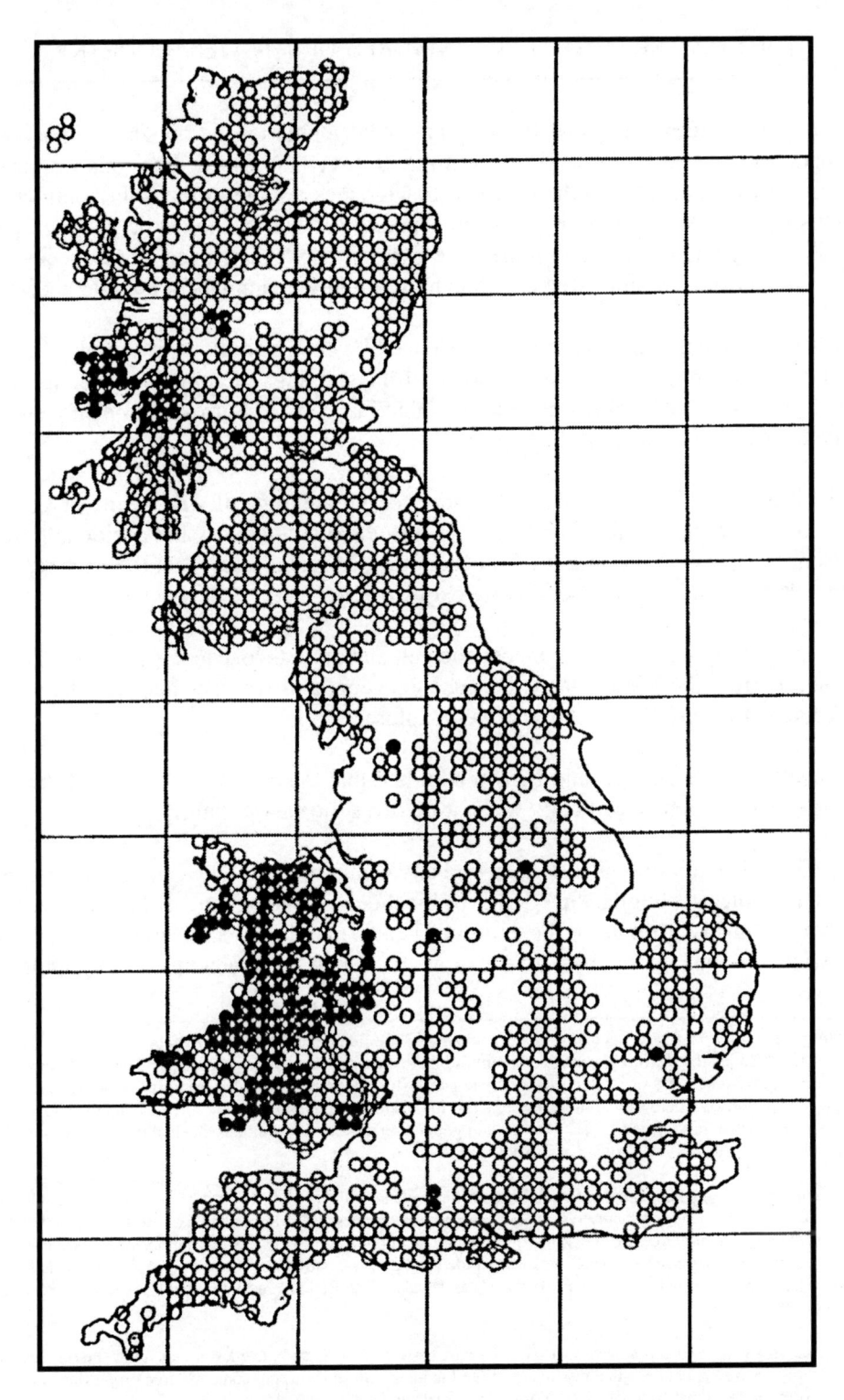

A map showing polecat populations on Forestry Commission land in the mid 1980's
(Note: Animals living outside Forestry Commission Land are not included)

THE SMALLER MYSTERY CARNIVORES OF THE WESTCOUNTRY

interbred with the remnants of the original wild population before the original wild population disappeared. However, intermittently over the succeeding years a genetic pattern which produces morphological characteristics unique to the wild strain comes to the surface. Therefore, animals of one species (or which should be more properly described as being complex introgressive hybrids between two or more species) are found which exhibit characteristics found more usually in animals of another species.

This is not to say that this theory of 'existence by genetic dilution' is completely invalid. I have used it myself to explain some of the sightings of animals which appear to be wild boar, (see footnote) which have been sighted in parts of Surrey, Hampshire and the Home Counties over the past thirty years.

Whilst it is probably that some of the more recent sightings of wild swine in England and Scotland are the result of deliberate re-introduction attempts, and accidental escapees from farms where they are bred for their meat, it seems likely that the ones reported in the 1960s and 1970s may be of more exotic origins.

There is no need, however, to concoct such an elaborate theory to explain the sightings of polecats from the Westcountry, because the genetic differences between the domesticated and wild varieties are far less well explored!

As recently as 1985, Porter and Brown admitted that the precise taxonomy of the mustelidae was uncertain, specifically when it involves the weasel family.

They admit that, not only is it hard to find any differentiation between certain strains of ferrets and polecats, but the knowledge of biochemical and genetic differences between the two animals is arbitrary in the extreme. This is mainly down to small differences in the facial markings on the mask of the creature, which, even amongst wild populations

---

1. Writing in *British Animals Extinct within Historic Times* (1880), Edmund Harting wrote about 'forest pigs' in the New Forest, which interbred with the semi-feral animals released each spring by local farmers. He described how the offspring of these unions were very reminiscent of wild boar which had been extirpated from Britain some years before. In an unpublished article which, sadly, became lost in the ether when my Amstrad PCW gave up the ghost in 1994, I suggested that these 'forest hogs', were a small population of truly feral animals that had lived in the New Forest since the days when truly wild swine had lived there.

I suggested that these regularly interbred with the semi-feral animals which - when Harting was writing - were let out for much of the year to fend for themselves in the same way that ponies on Dartmoor and Exmoor (and indeed in the New Forest) have a semi-wild existence. I theorised that a relict population of these beasts still existed in the 1990s, and occasionally produced a throwback which was almost identical to a true wild boar. This would explain the wild boar sighted in Hampshire during the 1960s and 1970s, as described by Bob Rickard and John Michell in their book *Living Wonders* (1982).

Now, however, we have *bona fide* wild boar back in many parts of the UK, and the question must now be regarded as unanswerable. However, I believe that my theory of feral animals whose gene pool contains large proportions of genetic material from a wild animal from which the domestic animals derived, is a good one.

American Mink (*Mustela vison*)

of polecats, can vary widely (the range of colouration morphs within the domestic ferret is enormous).

The real problem is that the mammalogical establishments have the intransigent attitude that, because they believe that polecats are extinct in the wild in England, therefore, all creatures which appear to be wild English polecats are, actually, ferrets.

When someone like Rennie Bere wrote of a polecat-ferret seen near Launceston in March 1969, and says that, although it was 'unusually dark' for a ferret, it 'could not have been mistaken for a polecat', in the light of the evidence we have already seen, a statement such as this is meaningless.

For those people who thought that this was purely a zoological riddle, there is one final twist, during which an element of phenomenological synchronicity enters the field.

- THE SMALLER MYSTERY CARNIVORES OF THE WESTCOUNTRY -

The concept of acausal synchronicity - unexpected and unexplained coincidences, whose mathematical improbability defies rational explanation, was first discussed by Karl Jung [36] early in the 20th Century, and many researchers including Colin Wilson, [37] have continued his theorising. In my experience, life, and especially the part of my particular life which is involved in fortean research, is full of such surreal synchronitic stupidity.

On the 12th April 1992, at about four in the afternoon, I telephoned Dr. Turk at the Institute for Cornish Studies, for information about polecat sightings in the county. She gave the information related a few pages ago, we chatted cheerfully for a few minutes and then the phone call ended with her promising to write to me with photocopies of all the Cornish records that she could find.

A week or so later I received a letter from her, containing a new sighting of polecats in Cornwall, the first for fifty years, [38] which had occurred on the very day that I had telephoned Dr. Turk and at exactly the same time!

Whether this means anything, I have no idea, and as a true fortean I make no judgements, but merely include the incident in this book as a minor example of what both

- THE SMALLER MYSTERY CARNIVORES OF THE WESTCOUNTRY -

Loren Coleman and the late Mark Chorvinsky describe as the 'high strangeness' that permeates all fortean zoological research, even when it is essentially only an attempt to clear up a minor zoological anomaly.

The 1992 record was of a pair of animals seen by Mrs. Barbara Holt at Luddock Wood in Cornwall. She described them as 18 inches in length with a long, bushy tail. The back was dark, whereas the face had a very distinct mask over the eyes and a white muzzle. They came out of a hedge playfully chasing each other. Mrs. Holt unerringly identified them as polecats!

After the evidence we have examined, only one thing is certain. There is no real way that anyone can tell the difference between a ferret and a polecat. Phil Drabble, the popular naturalist wrote in 1976: [39]

> "A few years ago scientists claimed that they could differentiate between a ferret and a polecat if they could examine the skulls. Then they found that if a 'Polecat' was fed on soft food – milk and bread for example – from the time it was weaned, and if a 'ferret' was flesh fed in an open pen with plenty of exercise, then the differences would be reversed".

The description of a 'ferret' as having a smaller and narrower skull than a 'polecat' becomes even less tenable when one discovers that until immediately before the First World War there was a race of 'Polecat' living wild in Sutherland, in the north of Scotland, which was notable for its narrow skull. [40] (see footnote)
Drabble continues:

> "My personal opinion is that there are no true Polecats left in the British Isles, assuming that there ever was any real difference between 'ferrets' and 'polecats'. They interbreed so freely that any ferret lost on a day's rabbiting would cross with its wild cousins if it survived long enough to fend for itself in the wild". [41]

---

1. The Sutherland polecat has been presumed extinct for over a century now, but it would not surprise me at all if a concerted effort to find one, even now, would produce a small population. The interesting thing about the Sutherland polecat, is that it was adapted for a semi-subterranean existence. Dr Karl Shuker, writing in *Mysteries of Planet Earth* (1999) wrote about a Scottish mystery beast known as the 'earth hound'. The earth hound or yard pig was described as being "about the size of a ferret" and having a head like a dog. These animals reportedly live underground in graveyards where they feast on fresh human flesh from the corpses buried therein.

Whereas the idea that an animal has evolved purely to feast off human flesh in graveyards is ludicrously unlikely, the idea that there is a second species, or subspecies, of mustelid in Scotland that has evolved to hunt moles and other creatures which dwell beneath the ground, is - to this author at least - not unlikely at all. These animals are only known from Banffshire (as far as we know), and I would suggest that they are seen predominantly by gravediggers, because it is only this group of people who habitually dig deep holes in the area where these animals live.

The CFZ is planning an expedition to Banffshire, complete with an array of Longworth Small Mammal Traps. We hope that we may be able to lay this particular mystery to rest.

Pine Marten (*Martes martes*)

Picture courtesy of Tom Anderson, photographed by Michael MacGregor

and he concludes:

> "*I think that 'ferrets' are merely 'polecats' made tame by centuries of domestication*". [42]

This is a conclusion with which I concur in full. Having kept a number of 'ferrets' over the last five years, including albinos, one specimen which seemed identical with the long extinct 'Sutherland polecat' and several whose markings and morphology made them indistinguishable from wild 'polecats', I can see no reason to argue.

There is no doubt in my mind that some ferrets have gone wild across the region, but I also have little doubt that they have interbred with the remnants of the original wild population to produce a new and healthy mustelid whose population is gaining strength and numbers throughout the region.

There was always a place in the ecosystem for a small to medium sized diurnal carnivore and the new arrivals have merely filled the gap left vacant with the decline of the original wild population. As we have seen, there is so little difference between ferrets and polecats as to make them practically indistinguishable and, therefore, there are, as there always have been, Polecats living wild in the Westcountry, and especially in Cornwall. The exact provenance of the gene pool is uncertain, but if nothing else, the so-called extinction of the species in England is just another manifestation of intransigent scientific short-sightedness.

Animals that appear to be polecats are becoming more common across the whole of the British Isles. In the mid-1980s, there were only a few records of putative polecats outside the areas of Wales, where their existence has never been in doubt. A map, reproduced on the next page, was originally published by a Forestry Commission survey into the distribution of certain mammals and birds across the land they own and administer. This shows that, even in the mid-1980s, there were a few pockets of polecat population predating the recent population explosion!

In 1994, the National Museum of Scotland launched a research project in an attempt to discover the true identity of polecat-like animals from England and Scotland, by means of genetic analysis of material recovered from road kill victims. At the time of writing, in the early summer of 1996, no results have been made public, but the species, at least as far as we can gather from eyewitness accounts, and the burgeoning number of road kills, seems to be increasing its range, and population, in an extremely encouraging manner!
There are two minor matters that perhaps merit discussion.

Several writers, including Hurrell himself, [43] mention the widespread belief that ferrets can hybridise with stoats. The stoat (*Mustela erminea*) is, as we enter the new millennium, the second most common carnivore in Britain after the fox. [44] It is also, by nature of its size and habits, one of the most cryptic, and it is seldom seen except by the most ardent naturalist. In the summer of 1994, I saw the first living wild stoat that I had seen for years running along the side of a road just outside Glastonbury. A year later, we saw another animal near the village of Sherfield on Lodden a few miles north of Basingstoke. Since then I have seen at least a dozen stoats at various places around the country. It appears, from reports we are receiving, as well as from our personal experience, that the stoat, like the polecat, is presently undergoing somewhat of a population explosion! There seems no reason why these two animals, so closely related, should not hybridise, either in captivity or in the wild, but despite several quite well publicised references, I can find no record of this actually occurring. [45] (See Appendix Two).

It has also been suggested that either the 'ferret' or the 'polecat' could hybridise with the mink. [46]

The American mink (*Mustela vison*) is one of the most common medium-sized carnivores in Britain today. The history of its gradual entry into the ranks of British mammalia deserves to be recounted here, if only as an example of how insidious mustelids can be, and how an animal, which forty years ago would have been well within the cryptozoological fauna of the region, has now become well-known and is even regarded as a pest.

For some reason that must remain a mystery for the moment, it is the American mink rather than its close relation, the European mink (*Mustela lutreola*) that has been commonly kept on fur farms since about 1929.

The two species are very similar, although the American species is slightly larger. [47] The European mink has not been a native of Britain, at least since the last Ice Age, and although it is still found in parts of Eastern Europe, and even in France, it is becoming gradually rarer across its range.

The American mink, however, is a very successful predator. It has a long, slender body slung low. It has short ears set close together, a bushy tail and short legs with toes partly webbed together. The thick fur is uniformly thick dark brown, with a small white spot on the lower lip. There are sometimes scattered white hairs, or even a few white spots, on the underside of the body. Numerous colour mutations have been obtained in captivity, but it appears that the animals soon revert to the wild colouration when they establish feral populations.

The head and body length is between 302 – 430 mm and there is an additional 127 – 229 mm of tail. The animals are mostly nocturnal, but I have seen them hunting by day. They proved themselves extremely adept at escaping from their, often badly run and unlicensed fur farms, and soon after the Second World War, rumours started to abound that the animals were breeding in the wild. [48]

It wasn't until 1953, however, that a water bailiff on the River Teign reported that it was almost devoid of rats because of a small, but thriving, colony of mink, and over the next six years reports began to pour in, not only from Devon and Cornwall, where it soon became apparent that the animals were far more widespread than had initially been thought, but from all over the British Isles. [49]

By the mid-1960s, 'the powers that be' realised that the species was so firmly entrenched that there was now no hope of eradicating the species within the country. It seems that one of the major reasons for the animals' success is its wide and unspecialised diet.

There is no real evidence to support the claims that its presence within the ecological infrastructure of the British countryside harms, in real terms, either mankind or any of the indigenous carnivores. Its habits and preferred food are different enough to either the otter or any other British species, for that matter, to suggest that even if these animals were to reach their pre-persecution numbers, the European mink could peacefully co-exist with them.

One lesson can be learned from the mink in this country and that is that they were almost completely entrenched within our fauna before anyone noticed that they were there in any numbers. This bodes ill for our native species, but well for whatever alien species will be the next to arrive.

During the summer of 1992, I visited a poacher in Launceston. He showed me some animals in a shed in his garden that he claimed were a cross between mink and polecat-ferrets. He certainly kept both species, and the animals that he showed me seemed to be unusually dark. Unfortunately, he refused all my offers of cash, and was adamant that he would not part with any of his animals. I tried to contact him a few years later, but it appeared that he had disappeared from the area and that no-one knew where to find him.

If the polecat and the mink *can* successfully hybridise, and there is little additional evidence to suppose that they do, it would be interesting to discover whether they have ever done so in the wild. [50]

We are in the odd position in the Southwest that the two most common medium-sized carnivores are both ones whose status provides interesting implications for the fortean zoologist. If they were to hybridise and add yet another bizarre creature to the fauna of the region, it would be a charming irony of which Charles Fort would, I am sure, totally approve.

- CHAPTER THREE -
THE PINE MARTEN

"Does history record any instance in which the majority was right?"

Lazarus Long

The pine marten, *Martes martes,* is arguably the most attractive, and certainly the rarest of the acknowledged British carnivores.

As is the case with so many of the mustelids, both the size and the colouration are variable. The total length can be anything from 630 mm to 760 mm, of which between 250 – 280 mm is tail. The animals are usually about 150 mm high at the shoulder and weigh between 0.9 and 1.5 kg. The females are, on the whole, slightly smaller than the male. [1]

The colour varies from a rich, warm brown to almost black on the upper parts and undersides. There is a creamy white throat patch or bib, often tinged with orange, and sometimes extending up to both sides of the neck. In some populations, this 'bib' is in two separate parts. The creature has a lithe, long body with short legs, sharp claws and a broad triangular head with a pointed muzzle and prominent ears with pale edges. The animal has large, black, prominent eyes.

There are scent glands near the base of the tail, but they do not smell as unpleasant as the contents of those of the polecat. A polecat at rest has quite a pleasant musky smell, but when frightened or attacked it voids its scent glands with very noxious results, resulting in its country name of 'Foumart' (Foul Marten). The pine marten, in contrast, is called the 'Sweet Marten'. [2]

The summer moult is from late spring to June with the winter moult starting in September or October. The natural range of the pine marten is across all the wooded parts of Europe from the Mediterranean to the limits of tree growth. It is also found in parts of Asia and closely related species are found in the rest of Asia and North America.

Until recent times, its fur has been of economic importance and it has been widely trapped. Indeed, it is uncertain whether its commercial value or its reputation as a predator of domestic livestock and game contributed most to its decline in the wild. It has been kept on fur farms for its pelt, but in general it does not do particularly well as a ranch bred animal. There are records of it being domesticated as a 'house pet' on some of the Greek islands, [3] and it has been kept in captivity in Britain on a number of occasions, notably by the Devon naturalist, H.G. Hurrell. [4]

Hurrell's daughter, Elaine, suggested that the animals kept as house pets in Crete were probably beech martens, rather than pine martens, and at the time of writing I have not been able to confirm either claim.

Although Langley and Yalden [5] state that this animal was hunted to extinction by 1834 in Surrey, and by 1830 – 50 in Hampshire, there have been a well documented series of sightings in Surrey over the past thirty years or so and this relict population has even been the subject of a popular children's book, *Fire in the Punchbowl*, by Monica Edwards. [6] An excerpt from this book describes the animal in matter-of-fact terms, without undue sensationalism:

> "...Then suddenly, too quickly to see it clearly, something came darting down a tree trunk. It was bigger than a squirrel and sandy coloured. It had a long body and a bushy tail. Some kind of rare foreign squirrel, Roger thought, gazing as it came cautiously over the soft pine-needles. It moved in quick, brief rushes, looking everywhere, half eager, half afraid, and then began to eat, with obvious enjoyment the food that Lindsey had put down. Suddenly in a flurry it was gone. Perhaps it had sensed that he was there..."

Miss Edwards was, as any aficionado of her books will verify, a meticulous observer of wildlife. Her descriptions of animals have always been factual in the extreme, and there seems no reason to believe that this episode in her story-book was not based on a true event!

In Hampshire, I have a probable record from the late 1980s, when an animal which appears to be of this species, was reported by some schoolboys on an 'Outward Bound' course in the New Forest. [7]

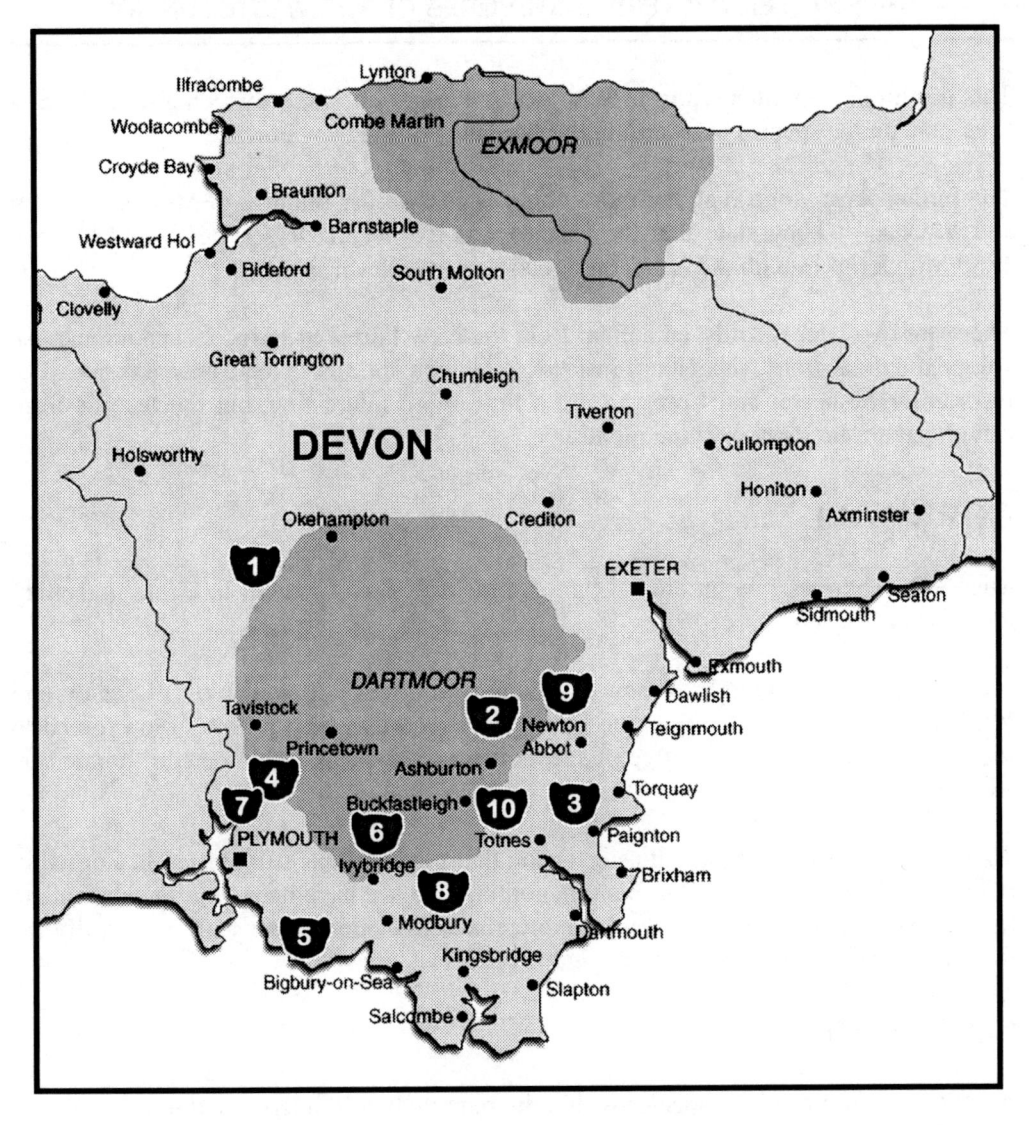

A Map of Devon showing the locations of pine marten sightings between 1918 and 1970

Key:

1. Lynford
2. Buckland in the Moor
3. Paignton
4. Piles Copse
5. Noss Mayo
6. Brentmoor
7. Maristow
8. Gnaton
9. Puslinch
10. Hurrell's home at South Brent

This ties in nicely with a report in Whitlock's *Wildlife of Wessex*, which also includes a brief note on the species in an account of the fauna of the New Forest. [8]

The further west you travel, the more doubt is cast on the findings of Messrs. Langley and Yalden. [9] They state that the species was extinct in Dorset, between 1800 and 1850, which ties in with the last certain record in my files from 1848. [10]

There are two later records, an animal from the New Forest in 1916, [11] and a creamish coloured animal from Abbotsbury in 1951, [12] which appears to have been a ferret. The records for Somerset and Cornwall are a little more interesting, but the records from Devon paint a far more exciting picture.

CORNWALL

Miss S.B. Andrews saw an animal that she identified as a marten in a tree in Tehidy Park during the summer of 1932.

As will be seen in the light of new evidence which was not available to Langley and Yalden, I am prepared to accept the Devonshire records which follow. I am forced to regard this sighting with a degree of scepticism as it appears not to be corroborated by any further evidence. [13]

There have been several rumours suggesting that pine martens still existed in Cornwall, at least until fairly recently, but there is nothing that we have been able to substantiate to any degree at all. Until we receive more concrete evidence, we shall, regretfully, be forced to consider the species extinct in the county!

SOMERSET

An 1861 report placed the species within the mammals of Somerset and there was a record of:

> "something that appeared to be a pine marten"

from Luckwell Bridge on Exmoor 'during the winter of 1924'. [14] This, again, seems on the surface of it to be an isolated incident, but we shall return to the martens of Exmoor later. (See Appendix Three).

DEVONSHIRE

In the 1977 edition of *Dartmoor*, (New Naturalist series), Ruth St. Leger-Gordon noted:

- THE SMALLER MYSTERY CARNIVORES OF THE WESTCOUNTRY -

Red Squirrel (*Sciurus vulgarius*)

> *"There are very few records of martens in Devon. Brooking Rowe in 1862 said that he knew of no recent records but quoted J.C. Bellamy for the statement that it lived in the woods in Lydford and Buckland-in-the-Moor".* [15]

There is no shortage of historical evidence for the existence of the species within the county but unlike the neighbouring counties, there is a great deal of evidence to suggest that this species survived well past 1900.

A comprehensive rundown of sightings was made in 1953 by the renowned Devon naturalist, H.G. Hurrell, who appears, as one digs further, to be the pivotal character in this whole saga. As will become evident during this chapter and the following one, I believe that Hurrell was a remarkable man and a fine naturalist. Immediately prior to completing this book I sent a copy of the final draft to his daughter, herself an eminent mammalogist, for her comments. Miss Hurrell does not approve of this book and took great exception to much of it. She described one particular paragraph as *"virtually libellous"*, *and* made a number of changes to my manuscript. I have included these changes where it appears that my original data was wrong, and in each case when she has objected to a

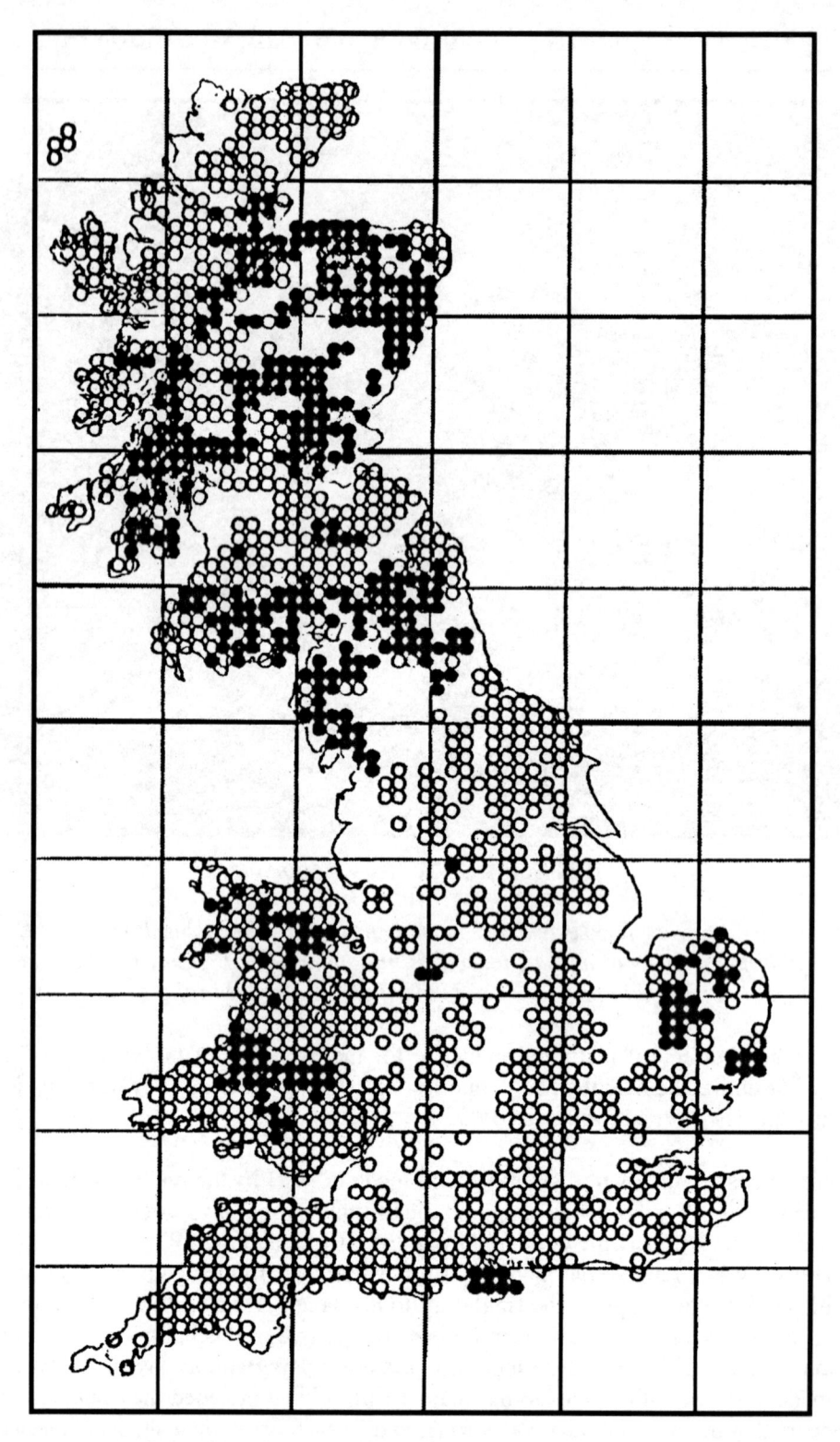

The distribution of the Red Squirrel (*Sciurus vulgarius*) in 1983

Red Squirrel (*Sciurus vulgarius*)
exhibited at the visitor centre Blue Pool, Furzebrook, Dorset

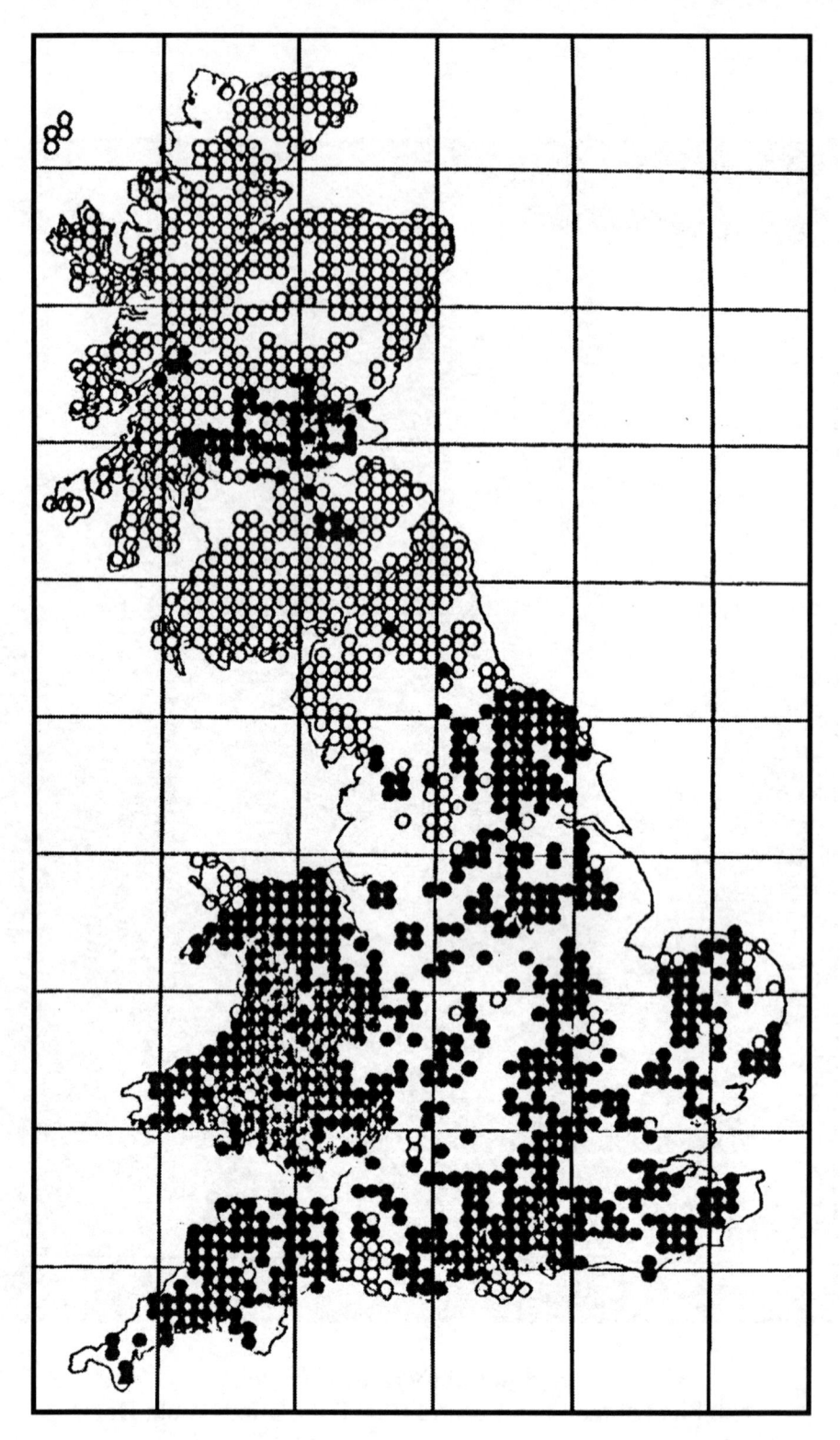

The distribution of the Grey Squirrel (*Sciurus carolinensis*) in 1983

certain passage, I have included her objections in the final work. I have not, however, deleted the passages to which she objected. In the interests of free speech, and also because my solicitor has told me that one cannot, in fact, 'libel' a dead person, I have not changed the main body of my arguments, and must reiterate that, despite her protestations, this book contains the results of my research. The conclusions that I have drawn are the ones which seem logical from the data I have presented.

Miss Hurrell objected to my sentence reading that *"H.G. Hurrell ... appears as one digs further to be the pivotal character in this whole saga"*. She instead wished me to write that *"H.G. Hurrell recorded in the Transactions of the Devonshire Association the reported sightings in Devon"*. I have not acceded to her wishes, not out of 'bloody mindedness', but because, unless I have totally misinterpreted the evidence available to me, Hurrell was the pivotal character in the whole affair!

His 1953 rundown of Devonshire pine marten sightings read as follows:

> *"Mr. Rossiter of Paignton tells me that he is convinced that he saw a pine marten near Paignton, in about 1918. Another reliable observer, Mr. Prior of St. Albans, claims to have seen a marten in Piles Copse, Dartmoor about the middle of 1932. One was seen very clearly at Noss Mayo, River Yealm in June 1952 by Major Brenda Gough.*
>
> *Several times an animal was glimpsed at night at Brentmoor House during 1952. There are reasons for thinking that it may have been a marten. Mrs. Weeks of Yelverton, and her son, suspect that they saw a marten in a high fir tree at Maristow in April 1953"*. [16]

Three years later, Hurrell wrote again:

> *"Mr. V. Almy has come across references to this species at Puslinch, Yealmpton in 1843 and 1860. Mr. O.D. Hunt reports that his sister saw one at Guaton near Newton Ferrers on July 11th 1955. It crossed the road in front of their car .. "* [17]

One was seen in Combeinteignhead on the 26th November 1972, [18] and another was seen there a year earlier, implying that this cryptic animal may well have been well established in the area at that time. [19]

> *"Boxing Day 1971. I saw a pine marten on top of my budgerigar aviary, having been attracted by the noise of the birds. The animal ran off at my approach. Its identification is not in doubt, because I have kept mink and I can state positively that the animal was a marten."*

This sighting is particularly interesting. The fact that the animal was seen on a budgerigar aviary implies that it may well have been used to people, and was, therefore, not afraid to approach human habitation.

Another animal was seen by R.M. Jewson in 1973: [20]

> "Denham Bridge, River Tavy 8.9.73. I was fortunate enough to spot an animal moving through the top branches of a high oak tree and then to some more oaks. At first I naturally suspected a squirrel but it was far too big for a squirrel whilst the tail was far too bushy for a mink. Also, it was dark brown or red – certainly not black. It took flying leaps from tree to tree with great agility.
>
> Having seen HGH's (Hurrell's) ranch bred pine martens when they were allowed to climb trees in a wood at Wrangaton I concluded that the animal I saw was indeed a pine marten. The leaps from tree to tree were quite considerable and it was fascinating to watch its performance".

The description of the animal leaping 'from tree to tree' is very important. It is one of the most notable facets of pine marten behaviour and it is one which we shall be returning to later in this chapter.

More recently, in a report from Wembworthy on the 20th February 1978 made by Mr. P. M. Stark:

> "8 a.m. An animal was seen in the trees of a coniferous wood running along the branches and going from tree to tree by jumping from the end of one branch to the nearest branch of the next tree. I could not see its colour against the light but it definitely had a bushy tail and appeared to be slightly larger than a squirrel. so I feel bound to conclude that it must have been a marten. Knowing that size can be difficult to estimate I have carefully reconsidered my assessment, but I still feel that it was definitely too big for a squirrel".

An animal that looked very much like pine marten was seen ten years later in August 1988 by Mr. Flemming of Exeter. He was driving his family towards Fingle Bridge for a day's outing, when they got hopelessly lost in the sunken Devon lanes. [22]

Suddenly an animal the size of a large cat jumped into the road in front of them and ran up the road before them with the car following at about the same speed. Mr. Flemming is interested in natural history, and was confused at what he saw because he was aware that pine martens are not supposed to be found in Devon.

- THE SMALLER MYSTERY CARNIVORES OF THE WESTCOUNTRY -

He described a long, sinuous dark red-brown beast which undulated along the road towards him. On a visit to Wales soon afterwards he visited a wildlife park and compared what he had seen with every animal that he could find, including pine martens and polecats, and he was convinced that what he had seen was a marten.

His only misgiving was that the animal had not seemed to possess the ubiquitous fawn throat patch or bib, and had seemed to be a uniform colour all over. This, as we shall see in the next chapter, is nowhere near as negative a piece of evidence as it would at first seem.

Three years later, on the 4th October 1991, Mr. Nettley of Bag Tor House, Ilsington heard his wife call him to see a strange animal that was climbing a tree at the end of his drive. [23]

The animal had disappeared by the time his wife had taken him to the tree in question, but she gave a clear description of a long, thin, squirrel-like animal about two feet in length, and with a reddish-grey colouration. She immediately identified the creature as a pine marten from a book on British wildlife.

Mr. Nettley discussed the incident with a number of people, all of whom said that what his wife had seen must have been a squirrel. His father-in-law however, an ex-policeman, told him that sometime within the previous thirty years a pine marten had been shot near Honiton by a farmer protecting his chickens.

Mr. Nettley also asked me if I could solve another mystery that had been puzzling him and several of his friends. Apparently, a number of them had been shooting in the thick deciduous woods in the immediate area, and they have occasionally heard the 'bangs and crashes' of a fairly large and invisible creature chasing something in the branches above them. These noises are regularly punctuated by the sound of the creature (if it is a creature) plummeting to the ground and are then followed by silence. He has experienced this phenomenon over a number of years, as have a number of his acquaintances, and he was extremely interested in finding out what the cause may have been.

Writing in 1968 in a booklet entitled pine martens which was published by the Forestry Commission, [24] H.G. Hurrell noted that this is the sound made by a marten whilst hunting a squirrel from tree to tree, a hunt which culminates with a crash as hunter and hunted fall to the ground:

> "I have heard of forestry workers in the north of England who could tell when a marten was present by the noise of a tree-top squirrel hunt. The possibility of detecting a marten in this way is supported by an eyewitness account given me by the late G.P. Ross, of a hectic chase in Germany in

which he had seen a red squirrel fleeing before a pine marten. The terror-stricken squirrel was leaping from tree to tree with the marten in close pursuit. At times they were lost to sight among the trees as they went further away. Even then they could still be heard as they crashed at full speed through unstable branches. The chase went on for some minutes until the marten seemed to be closing upon the tiring squirrel. They were in full view again when with a final leap the marten seemed to catch the squirrel in mid-air. Both fell to the ground and the marten proceeded to make a meal of its victim".

A tree-top chase like the one described by Hurrell would I feel, be the ideal explanation for the mysterious noises described by Mr. Nettley, and in the absence of a better explanation, I would like to suggest this as the truth behind them.

I have reports of similar sounds from several sites within a ten-mile radius of the 1991 sighting at Ilsington, [25] and in my opinion, these can only be considered as positive supporting evidence.

The details of behaviour reported by all these observers are too similar to be coincidental. There are other interesting aspects to these reports as well.

Mr. Jewson's 1973 sighting was particularly significant in that he gave serious consideration to the possibilities that the animal that he saw could have either been a mink or a red squirrel (the two species most commonly confused in the wild with pine martens) but ended up rejecting both of these hypotheses in favour of the identity he chose. Pine martens, mink and red squirrels are really superficially very similar, but at the time Mr. Jewson made his report, red squirrels were practically extinct in the region, and he was very familiar with the appearance of mink.

The arrival of the American mink into the ranks of the British fauna was discussed in the previous chapter. The current status of the native British red squirrel (*Sciurius vulgaris*), also presents some interesting aspects for the cryptozoologist, and cannot be ignored by our investigation.

S. vulgaris has been in decline across most of its British range for most of the 20th Century. In the Westcountry it is generally considered to be extinct, except for two small colonies on islands off the Dorset coast. (See Appendix Three).

The red squirrel is not only quite similar in appearance to the pine marten, but also, in areas where the two species co-exist, it's main food source. The decline of the species in the Westcountry, in many ways mirrored the decline of the pine marten.

Writing in 1974, N.V. Allen noted that the species had been fairly common in the deciduous woods of the region until the severe winter of 1947, after which the species declined rapidly. [26]

Other writers have cited a mystery virus that supposedly decimated the species. Many other writers blame (not altogether unfairly) the far more successful grey squirrel (*S. carolinensis*), which was introduced from America in the late 19th Century. It seems probable, however, that the species was in decline long before the introduction of its transatlantic cousin. [27]

There are very few recent Devon records. These are all taken from the Mammal Reports in the annual *Transactions of the Devonshire Association*. They were present at Newton Ferrers as recently as 1962, but were quickly superseded by the introduced species. [28] Other reports are from Whitchurch Down on the 10.6.1965, [29] Tavistock on the 16.8.1966, [30] Yealmpton in October 1971, [31] and most recently Honiton on the 8.8.1972. [32]

In 1966, S.C. Madge wrote that the species was almost extinct in South-eastern Cornwall, although 'there still might have been a few at Mount Edgecombe'. [33]

Two years later, Dr. D.W. Turk wrote that:

> "Although local the species is still widespread in the county and may indeed be spreading into new areas". [34]

In 1979, Manning noted that:

> "It seems likely that the red squirrel has vanished from this part of England".

He expressed a faint hope that some might still survive in the far western tip of Cornwall. [35] There are a few other Cornish records in the archives of the Institute for Cornish Studies, but after the mid-1970s even these peter out. [36]

Officially, the status of the species is even less certain. Harry Pepper from the Forestry Commission Research Centre, says that the most recent Westcountry sightings that he is prepared to substantiate are from the edges of Bodmin Moor in 1965. His most recent records from Devonshire are a decade earlier than that! [37]

According to Mr. Pepper, the only remaining 'wild' specimens on the South western Peninsula are small populations on Brownsea and Furzey Islands off the Dorset coast. Even these have been 'propped up' by regular introductions of fresh stock, and are therefore not 'true' Westcountry animals.

There is a very common 'reddish bronze' phase of *S.carolinensis*, [38] and the two species are often confused. When I was living in Canada in 1979, it appeared that the most common phase of *S.carolinensis* was this reddish creature. The red squirrel had, ironically, been introduced into some of the major public parks by early English and Scottish settlers.

Having seen both *S.vulgaris* and the red phase of *S.carolinensis*, 'side by side', I can confirm that apart from the ear tufts (which are such a notable feature of the European species) the two animals are extraordinarily similar. My own observations in Toronto also cast doubt on the widely held belief that the two species are incompatible and cannot live in the same habitat.

Dr. S. Turk, of the Institute for Cornish Studies, told me in 1991 that every year they receive a large number of reports of *S.vulgaris* from the county. In the absence of corroborative evidence, however, she considers them to be specimens of the red phase of *S. carolinensis*. [39]

A newspaper report about a specimen that was recorded by the Institute for Cornish Studies in 1977 highlighted the confusion between the two species:

> "Perhaps the oddest sighting was that in St. Mary's Gardens, Falmouth, of a grey squirrel with a red tail. Such hybrids had been suspected but are very unlikely though, the experts say". [40]

It is reports like this which bring the collector of zoological anomalies into disrepute. Such a hybrid would be extremely unlikely, and there is no reason not to suppose that this is just another example of the red phase of *S.carolinensis*.

The only recent records worth consideration are both from the archives of the Institute for Cornish Studies: One animal was seen 'by the side of the road' near Tressilian in June 1984, by a person who claimed to be familiar with the differences between the two species. [41]

The other record of note is a little more intriguing. *The Western Morning News* of the 24th June 1983 reported the following story under the headline 'SQUIRREL IN SWIM'. [42]

> "The sudden appearance of a squirrel in St. Ives harbour yesterday astonished holidaymakers and fishermen. It was seen running in terror along Smeaton's Pier pursued by screaming gulls.
>
> The red squirrel fell off the end of the pier into the sea and then swam to dry land in the harbour. It was picked up by Mr. David McClary, a fisherman,

who put it in a van.

Later, when it dried out, it was taken to Tregenna Woods and released in the hope that it would join other red squirrels in the wood. Where it came from is a mystery".

There is a typewritten footnote by the bottom of the photocopy of this clipping in the Institute archives. It reads that:

"Mr. W.F.H. Ansell hopes to investigate the possibility that there is a colony of red squirrels at St. Ives/Carbis Bay". [43]

I telephoned Mr. Ansell in early 1992, but he told me that it is almost certain that no such colony actually exists. He also said that he is not prepared to accept any Cornish records of *S.vulgaris* since the mid-1970s. He is prepared to accept the vague possibility that there was a relict population on The Lizard, which provided the 1981 sighting, but said that it has probably now disappeared. [44]

In the Spring of 1992, Mr. Johnny Searles of Hartland saw a red squirrel in a forestry commission plantation just north of Woolsery in North Devon. [45] He was a countryman through and through. I knew him when I was a child, and although he is now dead, I am prepared to consider this record, anomalous though it undoubtedly is. [see footnote]

If there is a chance that red squirrels could have survived undetected in North Devon, could not pine martens also have done so?

A well-known North Devon Zoologist, who has asked to remain anonymous, told me that there is a small, but flourishing population of pine martens, some of which he has observed personally, in a small wooded valley on the edges of Exmoor. He also told me that he had received reports of 'mink that climbed trees' from elsewhere on Exmoor and that he felt that it was likely that these creatures were pine martens.

I have since received information that casts some doubt on the veracity of these reports. However, as they tie in nicely, both with the report from the Somerset portion of Exmoor quoted earlier, and with other information in my files, I have let them remain as part of my body of evidence. However, I would suggest that they are treated with caution. [46] At least two other wild populations appear to exist in the county; one just

---

1. The late Denny Braund, from Woolsery - which is now the home of the Centre for Fortean Zoology - told me that, as late as the early 1980s there were red squirrels in the woods above Bucks Mills, and that he believed there were also some in the Glebe woods attached to Clovelly Court Estate.

outside Teignmouth and one on the deeply wooded eastern edge of Dartmoor. Are these animals, however, the descendants of the original wild population?

Harvey and St. Ledger-Gordon, in their book *Dartmoor*, (1953) [47] which has already given us an interesting Polecat record, wrote that escapes of pine martens did indeed occur from various fur farms on Dartmoor and that not all of those animals had been recovered. They went on to say, however, that:

> *"They would certainly be able to support themselves quite well and it is possible that the animal seen at Piles Copse was one of these feral (sic) animals which had escaped from a farm in Chagford in 1921 or 1922".*

They also note from the escape records that the male and the female of the species were never loose at the same time, and so a chance of re-establishing the animal never occurred.

The same year, H.G. Hurrell remarked:

> *"There have been one or two escapes from Wrangaton since 1940 and one from Chudleigh in 1921. It is unlikely that the 1918 Marten could have been an escapee but those seen subsequently may have been".* [48]

I suspect that this is not actually the whole truth.

I do not want to appear critical of Hurrell. He was a naturalist for whom I have the highest regard, and from talking to people who knew him, I have discovered that he was an intelligent and gentle man.

He clearly had a charming and childlike enthusiasm for the species. He wrote a storybook about the adventures of a pine marten called 'Fling', based on his observations of pine martens both in captivity and in the wild. His other writings are also full of references to the species. He kept them as pets, and I think that it is unarguable that he loved the creatures very much.

I consider it highly likely that he helped the process of re-colonisation on a little by releasing specimens from his own captive breeding programme into the wild, to help bolster up the ailing wild population. I know that if I had been in the same situation, I would have done exactly the same thing.

As already noted earlier in this book, Hurrell's daughter has taken grave exception to much of what I have written about her father. When the penultimate draft of this book was complete, and we started to research the illustrations that we wanted to include, we felt that it would be nice to include a picture of Hurrell himself, preferably with one of his pine martens.

She, reasonably enough, asked to see a draft copy of the book. We sent it to her as requested, and were very upset when we read her comments. Much of this book was intended as an affectionate tribute to Hurrell; a man, whom we believe was almost solely responsible for saving the species in the wild in Devonshire. Unfortunately, it appears that she interpreted this book as an unprovoked attack on her family. It is nothing of the sort!

She objected to practically everything we had written about her father. She even scribbled through the line which read:

> "He kept them as pets, and I think that it is unarguable that he loved the creatures very much".

I find it hard to see what anyone could object to in a line like this.

She wrote:

> "All the individual martens that he trained to follow him outside their enclosures were accounted for. At no time did he deliberately release any martens into the wild. The widespread use of traps was one of the discouraging features".

She continued:

> "The suggestion that a release programme was carried out by him is totally inaccurate and speculation of this kind is not acceptable!"

As will be seen in the next chapter, several eminent zoologists have made claims to me about Hurrell's *modus operandi*, which directly contradict those claims made by his daughter.

What is certain, both from the evidence presented in this chapter, and in chapter four, is that feelings run high over the whole matter and that, as the main protagonist is dead, the exact truth of the episode may never be known!

Miss Hurrell was able to clear up one minor mystery however!

The inference from what Harvey and St. Ledger-Gordon wrote, [49] is that there were a number of fur farms in the area which kept the species. Hurrell obtained his first animals from a zoo, which was closing down. His animals had originally come from Germany, but it does appear that they were fairly widely available. Unfortunately, I had not been able to trace any of these fur farms, and approaches made to the Fur Breeders' Association had proved fruitless.

According to Miss Hurrell, there were only two fur farms in the area. One run by her father and one, the Peregrine Fur Farm run by John Stephenson, at Chagford.

Harvey and St. Ledger-Gordon seem to have had remarkable access to the records of the fur farm at Chagford, from which, it appears, several escapes took place. I have, unfortunately, had no luck in discovering more about this establishment.

It does seem, from other references in the available literature, including the one by Hurrell himself cited earlier, that there were martens, and indeed mink in other collections in southern Devon. What is also apparent is, that although some of these enterprises were not large enough to be worthy of the title of 'Fur Farms', there were several places where martens, mink and possibly other species were kept on a small scale for their fur, and escapes may well have occurred from some of these!

It is not actually certain, from what Miss Hurrell wrote, whether there were 'only two' establishments in the area (known to her) which were sizeable enough to be referred to as 'Fur Farms', or whether there were other fur farms that she knew of in the area, but that there were only the two which kept pine martens.

In either case, speculation is reasonably pointless because Hurrell himself referred [48] to an '*escape from Chudleigh*' in 1921, and that, despite what his daughter was to claim to us - forty-three years later - there had been '*one or two*' escapes from his collection at Wrangton, near South Brent, since 'about 1940'.

In both cases, Elaine Hurrell's claims that 'all the animals were accounted for', and that there were 'only two' establishments in the area that kept martens, have been contradicted by the testimony of her own father!

I spoke to Paul Blight at the Zoology Department of Bristol University who said:

> "*I am convinced that there has been no natural population of pine martens since the war*". [50]

but he agreed with me that any creatures still living in Devon were probably the descendants of those liberated by Hurrell.

At this point in my original manuscript, Miss Hurrell wrote:

> "*This is totally speculative, not to mention inaccurate*".

I felt that, in the interests of presenting all sides of the question, her comments here, and in a few paragraphs time, should be included!

I also spoke to the Devonshire naturalist, Kelvin Boot, who is also interested in the species. He, however, tends to discount the Devon sightings since about 1950 as being a mixture of misidentification and over-eagerness by a succession of Mammal Recorders for the Devonshire Association, (who were all members of the Hurrell family). [51]

I had originally claimed that from Hurrell's writings, both within the pages of the *Transactions of the Devonshire Association* and elsewhere, it seems that although he kept these animals for many years, he had very little success in actually breeding them in captivity. [52]

Miss Hurrell pointed out that:

> "This is also wrong. A number of litters were successfully reared. He found that they were not easy to breed in captivity, but even so a number of litters were reared successfully".

This was corroborated by Hurrell himself, who wrote: [24]

> "From 1939 to 1950 litters were produced and reared annually".

According to Hurrell, therefore, his breeding programme had ceased by 1950. Kelvin Boot told me, however, that during the 1950s and 1960s, Hurrell had attempted a structured reintroduction programme on Forestry Commission land, but he claimed that it was not a success. [53]

Miss Hurrell's comment on this claim was that:

> "This is totally untrue and appears to be a total invention without factual foundation!"

The evidence I have presented here suggests otherwise and it also suggests that this hypothetical reintroduction programme was, in fact, a success! Whether Hurrell knew this or not, it is impossible to say. This re-introduction programme was not well publicised, and I have been unable to discover any supportive evidence about it. From what I have been able to discover about Hurrell's character and *modus operandi*, it seems eminently likely.

Miss Hurrell wrote that this last statement of mine was '*virtually libellous*'. I disagree. Hurrell died in 1980, and under British law one cannot libel a dead person. Secondly, to be libellous a statement should be defamatory. This is not!
If Hurrell did indeed, as I believe, carry out a reintroduction programme, he was not

breaking any law by doing so. The Wildlife and Countryside Act (which, in any case, was only passed many years later) forbids the release of alien species into the British countryside. Pine martens are native to this country, and although the animals kept by Hurrell were of German origin, it seems almost impossible that, had they been public knowledge, his actions would have been considered illegal. The most important stumbling block to any legal objections to Hurrell's hypothetical reintroduction programme, is that the relevant legislation was not passed into law until a year after Hurrell's death, over a decade after the alleged introduction programme ended.

It seems almost impossible to consider that if Hurrell had been reintroducing pine martens to Forestry Commission land, he would consider doing so without permission. I have been told 'off the record', by various ex-forestry commission employees, that such permission would certainly have been (and probably was) granted.

The most important evidence to suggest that Hurrell was eminently capable of carrying out such an unorthodox and bold reintroduction scheme comes from his own writings. He was an unorthodox and bold naturalist who was never afraid to approach problems in a refreshingly unconventional style. Consider his description of what he described as 'liberty' pine martens: [24]

> "The martens (...) were my ranch bred animals which had been reared at my Devon home. They had been trained to come to a special device for food. At first they were encouraged to expect rewards of food in a pan which was attached to a long pole; a device which I called a 'martinet'. When trained in this way, they would eventually follow the pan and respond to it like a hawk to a lure. They would ascend trees when the pan was raised to the branches and they could be lured back from the wood to their nearby pens for their main feed. A little hawk bell was fastened to the pan so that it could be located by ear.
>
> Should a marten fail to respond and go off, it would fortunately almost certainly come back in its own time".

This type of husbandry is quite well known amongst bird-keepers. There are 'free flying', though captive, flocks of several members of the parrot family, and even such exotic creatures as night herons at various places in the British Isles, but to use this technique for mammals, especially as rare a carnivore as the pine marten is, as far as I am aware, unprecedented.

It can also be seen that Hurrell took techniques from falconry as well as aviculture and incorporated them into his own marten-rearing technique. Anyone capable of such brilliantly innovative thinking would be, in my opinion at least, perfectly capable of carrying out a secret reintroduction programme.

Pine Marten (*Mustela martes*)

- THE SMALLER MYSTERY CARNIVORES OF THE WESTCOUNTRY -

But why keep it secret?

Why not?

Miss Hurrell provided the most likely answer when she wrote:

> *"The widespread use of traps was one of the discouraging features".*

to Hurrell carrying out a reintroduction programme. Is it not more likely that the opposite is, in fact, true? I believe that Hurrell was a pragmatist and realised that only his actions could save the species in Devonshire. It was the 'widespread use of traps' that discouraged him from actually telling anyone about his programme. If it was to be a success, and it does appear that it probably was, then it would have to be kept a secret, and so kept secret it was. For the highest motives, Hurrell did not tell anybody of what was perhaps his greatest achievement. He also used Forestry Commission land because it was less likely to be poached, and therefore 'his' martens would have a greater chance of survival.

The ongoing series of sightings that have taken place intermittently ever since suggest that Hurrell's greatest legacy to the Devonshire countryside is still thriving!

On the 17th July 1982, the situation was complicated further when the Animal Liberation Front announced that they had liberated a pair of pine martens stolen from Paignton Zoo at an undisclosed location in the country. Nothing more has been heard about these animals in the successive three years. [54]

In an attempt to find out where these animals were liberated so that their progress in the wild could be monitored, I tried to contact the people responsible for their theft, but all my attempts at contacting a spokesperson from the Animal Liberation Front, who actually knew what he/she was talking about, have failed. By dint of pulling some rather grubby and disreputable strings, I eventually got to meet two cheerful, self-styled, Eco-terrorists in the Cavern Club in Exeter. Neither of them knew what a pine marten was! I bought them a beer and went home, slightly disappointed, knowing that this trail, at least, was closed for good.

As I write this during the summer of 1995, there seems little doubt that martens still live in Devonshire. Their provenance, however, is extremely questionable.

I have reasons to doubt the veracity of some of the records from the north of the county, and whilst I am sure that some of them are of martens, the exact identity of the Devon animals is still very much in question.

Over a decade after I wrote those words, I found myself sitting in a pub in a little village called Marston Trussell in rural Leicestershire. I was at a Big Cat Conference organised by Merrily Harpur, author of *Mystery Big Cats* (Heart of Albion, 2006). Sadly, she had been rushed to hospital the day before with a ruptured appendix, and yours truly had been brought in at the 11th hour to run the event. As always seems to be the case at these events, whilst the talks were entertaining and informative, the main business of the conference took place in the bar!

I was sat with my fiancée Corinna, and a bloke from Dorset called Jonathan McGowan. He had given a fascinating talk about big cats in Dorset, and it was obvious from the enormous portfolio of wildlife photographs that he carried with him that he was a field naturalist *par excellence!*

He had been pivotally involved in discovering the wild population of green lizards *(Lacerta viridis)* in Dorset, which proved to confirm a hypothesis that I had written about in the very first issue of *Animals & Men* back in 1994. However, the conversation turned to other unknown animal species in Dorset, and with a slightly embarrassed look on his face he leaned forward and said: *"You'll probably think I'm mad when I say this. Most people do. But I think that there are still pine martens in Dorset; and what's more, I think there might be another species as well..."*

I burst out laughing, and bought him a drink. At last I was not alone!

- CHAPTER FOUR -
OTHER MARTEN SPECIES

"If 'everyone knows something' then it 'aint so - not by a long way"

Lazarus Long

So far we have seen that far from becoming extinct in the 19th Century, even the most conservative zoologists will allow that the pine marten survived in Devonshire sixty five years longer than did Langley and Yalden, [1] and there is enough evidence to suggest that although the provenance is uncertain, there are wild pine martens in the county to this day.

The story is far from over, however, and it is now time to introduce a true cryptozoological element in the question.

Ian Linn, of the Zoology Department of Exeter University, and also a well-known Mammalogist agreed with my tentative theorising about pine martens in Devonshire, but added a bombshell of his own when he told me that he believed that the animals kept by Hurrell (and therefore presumably the animals liberated by him as well) were not the native species but the closely related American marten (*Martes americana*). [2] [3]

Miss Hurrell was adamant in her disagreement. She wrote on the original manuscript of this book:

Cranborne Chase, where according to many sources, there was a thriving fur industry, where *both* species of marten were harvested. Ironically, the beech marten seems to be the most common of the two species.

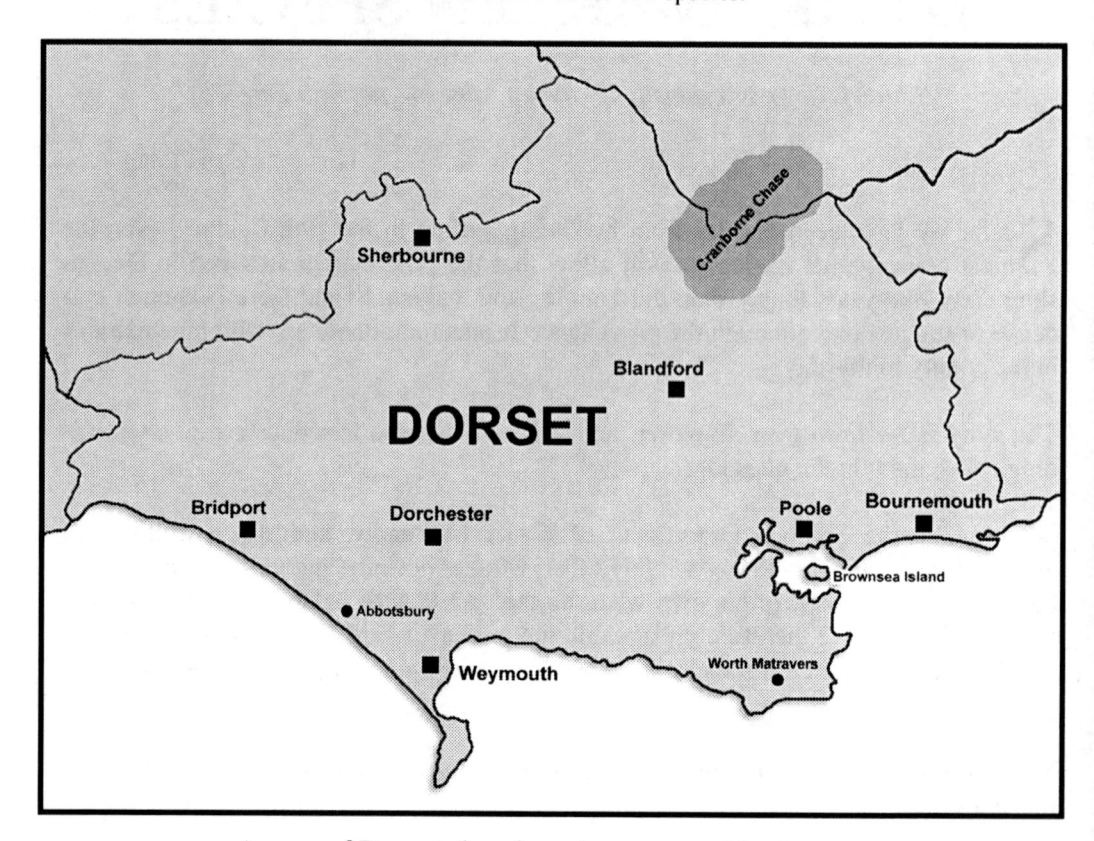

A map of Dorset showing places named in the text

- THE SMALLER MYSTERY CARNIVORES OF THE WESTCOUNTRY -

Mystery Marten displayed at the
Square and Compass, Worth Matravers, Dorset

During the preparation of this present volume, Mark North, the Assistant Director of the CFZ, and also the head of our Art Department, left the CFZ HQ in rural North Devon, and went back to his home in Dorset for a week. He spent the week travelling around the county collecting pictures for his book on Dorset folklore.

On his travels he found himself in a small museum in the village pub of Worth Matravers. As he always does, he took photographs of everything that he saw, and when he returned to the CFZ he showed me the pictures.

This is certainly a marten, but most interestingly, even from a side view, the `bib` which is characteristic of the pine marten was missing. Could this be a *bona fide* specimen of the Dorset beech marten? It is certainly a possibility, and when considered along with the other supporting evidence contained in this book, it paints a compelling picture to suggest that everything we know about the smaller carnivores of these islands is completely wrong!

"All this is totally inaccurate – the animals kept by my father were Martes martes – the pine marten without any doubt <u>whatsoever</u>".

There is no reason to doubt her word. Her father was a fine naturalist, and there is nowhere in his writings where he suggests that he ever kept the North American species. All the photographs of Hurrell's martens that I have seen are, as his daughter claims, undoubtedly pine martens, and as will be seen later in this chapter, the preserved animals in Westcountry museums are also undoubtedly of the species *Martes martes*. If it were not for Ian Linn's suggestion the matter would never even have been discussed and is included now only for the purposes of completeness.

It is, however, slightly disturbing to find that the American species is mentioned again, albeit tangentially, in conjunction with another mystery animal from Devonshire.

A little known report from the 1979 volume of the *Transactions of the Devonshire Association* merely served to confuse matters further. [4]

An extremely puzzling corpse was found on the road between Exeter and Exmouth, where it had obviously been knocked over by a car. [5] It was originally identified as a pine marten, but it was eventually found to be a beech marten, (*Martes foina*), a species that is not supposed to have existed in these islands since before the last Ice Age. [6] Despite the identification of the creature given in the *Transactions of the Devonshire Association*, Kelvin Boot is convinced that it was actually a specimen of *Martes americana*, which ties in nicely with what Ian Linn claimed on the previous page. [7][8]

The corpse, however, seems to have disappeared as so many important pieces of quasi fortean evidence are wont to do, and the matter for the moment must remain unsolved.

There is at least one more *M.foina* escapee from Devon in my files. Ian Linn told me of an animal which escaped from a private collection during the Second World War, and which lived wild in Devonshire for several years, before being found dead in a barn near the home of its original owner. [9]

M.martes and *M.foina* co-exist across much of their European range and there is little doubt that the species could easily live in Devonshire. The big question is, however, apart from two records of escapee specimens and one anomalous corpse, is there any reason to believe that the animal, which after all is not on the British list of resident mammals, was ever resident here? The answer, surprisingly, is 'yes'.

A paper on the mammals of Devon published by the Devonshire Association in 1877 includes the following species of mustelids as resident in the county. [10]
the polecat (*Putorious puro*), the pine marten (*Martes martes*) and the marten cat (*Martes foina*). I make no apologies for quoting this entry for *Martes foina* in full.

Comparison of the skulls of
Pine martin (*Martes martes*) and Beech Marten (*Martes foina*)

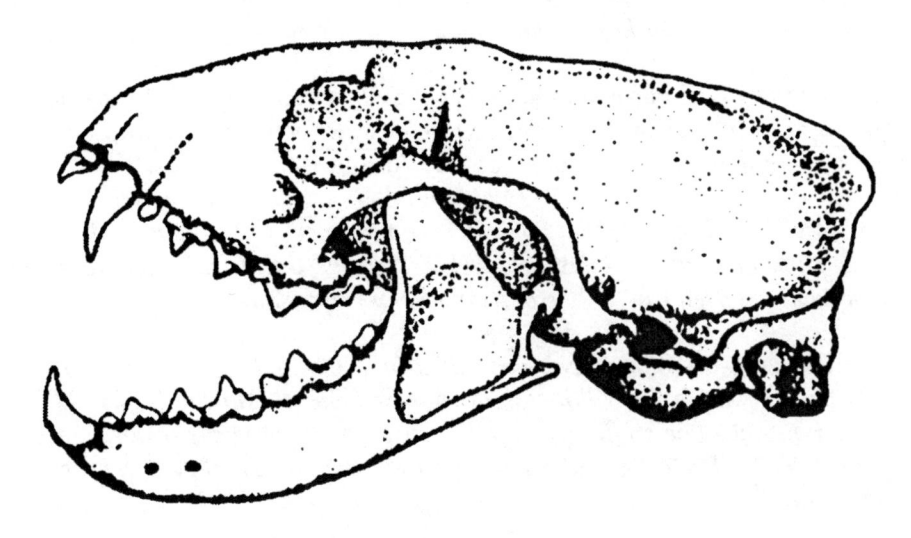

Pine martin (*Martes martes*)
Distance between the bullae in the region of the carotid foramina is more than half the length of the bulla from its interior end to the para-occipital process; length of bulla freater than the distance between the external edges of the jugular foramen

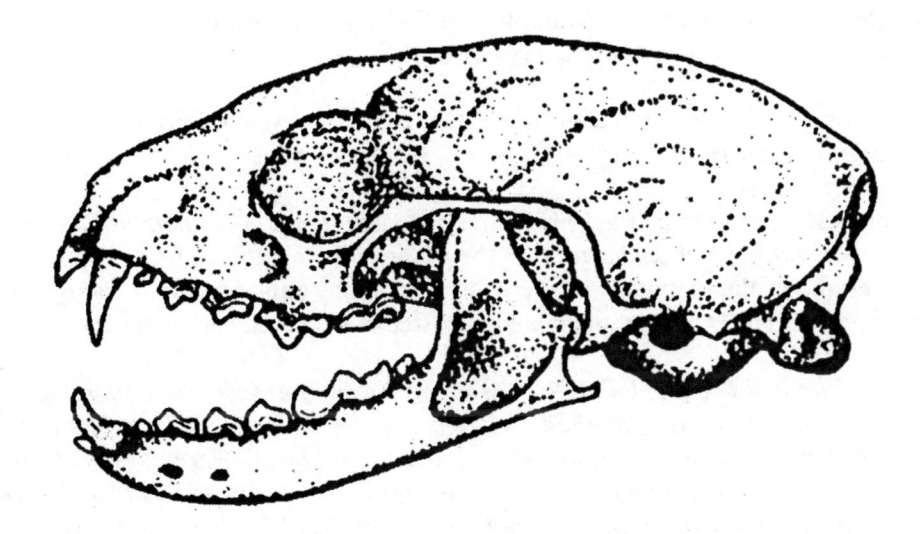

Beech Marten (*Martes foina*)
Length of the bullais less than (or occasionally equal to) the distance betwwen the external edges of the jugular foramen.

> *"This species is now, I believe, nearly extinct as a systematic war is waged against it by preserves of game. Mr. P.F. Amery informs me that the last he has heard of was killed near Ashburton about six years ago".*

Writing in 1897 in his paper on the *Destruction of Vermin in Rural Parishes*, which we quoted at length when discussing the polecat, Brushfield describes the status of martens as vermin in the Westcountry of the 17th and 18th Centuries: [11]

> *"MARTEN: There are but few entries on the Parish Accounts of their destruction and all varieties are included under one term. According to Bellamy 'Marten Cat' is one of its names in Devonshire.*
>
> *At Okehampton, a 'martyn' was killed in 1760, and a 'marteil' in 1787. Two were paid for at Wellington in 1609 and one (a 'Marting') in 1700. In each instance one shilling was paid. In 1744 'three marts heads' are entered in the Ecclesfield accounts but from the context they are probably foumarts".*

There are several pieces of useful corroborative evidence here. Firstly, Brushfield himself stresses that there is more than one species involved by stating that 'all varieties' are under consideration.

Secondly, although it could be suggested that the variety in names could be mere regional variation, the fact that two separate names were used in the same town only twenty-seven years apart, would imply that the townsfolk were used to dealing with two separate species and regarded them as such.

It is also interesting that as recently as 1897, Brushfield was referring to polecats by their country name of 'foumarts'.

It is interesting to note that a 19th Century account of the *Mammals of Somerset* includes *M.foina* but not *M.martes*, [12] (See Appendix Three). In Cornwall, too, an 1867 resume of the mammals of the county mentions only *M.foina*, although, as we have already seen, *M.martes* undoubtedly existed in the county at the time:

> *"'Rare and Local'. I do not know of any recent notices of its capture, and Mr. Crouch, writing in 1854, believed it to be no longer an inhabitant of the county. 'The last specimen', he says, 'I have been aware of, was killed near Liskeard in the first quarter of the present century, and its loss (for it was in ancient times classed with animals of the chase, and its fur was in high esteem), may be ascribed to the change of habits in society, by which the common use of mineral coal was introduced among farmers. Before that time a large number of pollard trees were permitted to grow in the*

neighbourhood of 'town places' or farm yards, for the purposes of supplying the house with fuel, and the cavities which most of them contained afforded a safe shelter to these, and the others of the weasel tribe. When such fuel became of less importance these hollow trees were gradually cut down, or suffered to fall, to the great diminution of the numbers of the weasel tribe". Report Royal Cornwall Polytechnic Society, 1854. pp.25, 25." [see footnote]

In a late 19th Century paper on the *Mammals of Dorset*, two species of marten are again mentioned. [15]

Again, I make no apologies for quoting the references, this time for both species in full!

"Marten Cat (Martes foina)

The Reverend William Chafin in his 'Anecdotes of Cranborne Chase', records Marten Cats as one of the animals hunted there but believes them (1816) to be nearly extinct, their skins too valuable for them to be allowed to exist. In 1836 one was caught alive near Stock House by the Rev. H.P. Yeatman's hounds but biting the huntsman's hands severely was kept alive for some time".

Whilst the entry for the pine marten merely read:

"One was shot near the Down House, Blandford by Sir John Smith's keeper in 1844". [14]

This places both species firmly within the Dorset fauna, and interestingly implies that *M.foina* was, at the time, the better known animal. A 1916 record of a Dorset pine marten is even more sceptical: [15]

"Mustela martes. (sic) The Pine marten. A record of this interesting little animal was sent in during the year but I am regretfully compelled to reject it for want of preciation (sic). As the animal has been recorded from Hampshire fairly recently the record is possibly correct but as the animal was only seen for a fairly short time and is unfamiliar I should prefer before admitting a record to see a skin of a Dorset specimen".

It was not until 1879, when Edward Alston published an article entitled *On the Specific*

---

1. The animal pictured on the next page is the only *bona fide* museum specimen of a Cornish pine marten that we know of. There may be other specimens in private hands, and we are still hopeful that we shall manage to locate them. My ex-wife and I travelled to Truro in June 1996 to root it out of the archives in Truro museum, and photograph it. It was our last excursion together.

The Pine Marten from Truro Museum
Is this the only 'true' Cornish Pine Marten in existence?

Identity of the British Marten [16] for the Royal Zoological Society, that what had hitherto been described as two separate species, became lumped together as one.

Within only a few years, the mammal reports of each of the regional societies that we have examined contained a sentence reading:

> *"Animals formerly supposed to belong to the species M.foina or marten cat are now considered to be Pine martens".*

Alston gave few reasons behind his decision to 'lump' the two species together as far as Great Britain was concerned. This was only one of several similar occasions in Victorian zoology.

Taxonomists were, and in some ways still are, either 'lumpers' or 'splitters' and in the days before Mitochondrial DNA analysis made the whole process of species definition a less arbitrary matter, were prone to 'lumping' together animals previously considered to belong to several different, though closely related, species into one larger species. 'Splitters', conversely created several 'new' species from one 'old' species on the basis of tiny, and often arbitrary differences. On many occasions during our researches, we have found animals described as individual species by Victorian explorers and zoologists, which now are not considered to be distinct even at sub-specific level.

In this case, however, the situation is somewhat different. Alston was not 'lumping' together two closely related species, but was, essentially, denying all the historical records of an animal, which as we have seen, were well-known to generations of naturalists, trappers, hunters and churchwardens. There is also no doubt, whatsoever, that *M.foina* was distinct at a specific level. Even Alston did not contest this, which makes his findings in this little known paper, which has, after all, shaped the face of British mustelid taxonomy for well over a century, all the more puzzling.

Even Alston's conclusions were not definitive, as he contradicted his own findings by noting one definite 19th Century record of *M.foina* from Northern Ireland. Unsurprisingly, when I contacted the mammal department at the British Museum (Natural History), they were adamant that they had no knowledge of any specimens of *M.foina* from the U.K. [17]

Alston also noted that even in 1879, martens (of whatever species) had an uncanny habit of turning up in areas where they had previously been considered extinct. [18]

> *"In the north of England, Mr. W.A. Durnford says the species is 'still plentiful', and in Lincolnshire several have been recorded, the latest, killed in 1865 by Mr. Cordeaux.*

The Pine Marten shot at Lynton, now displayed in the Ilfracombe Museum. This is probably the only *bona fide* Devon specimen that is on public display. All other specimens that we have managed to locate in Devon museums have been from Hurrell's collections, and are labelled as such.

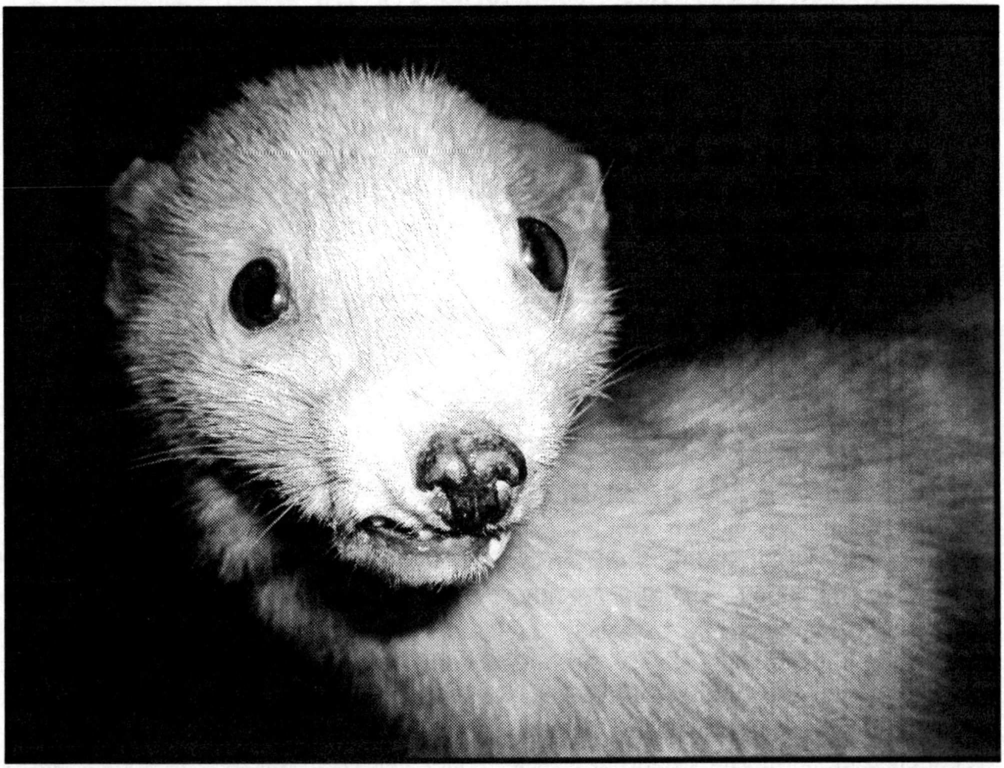

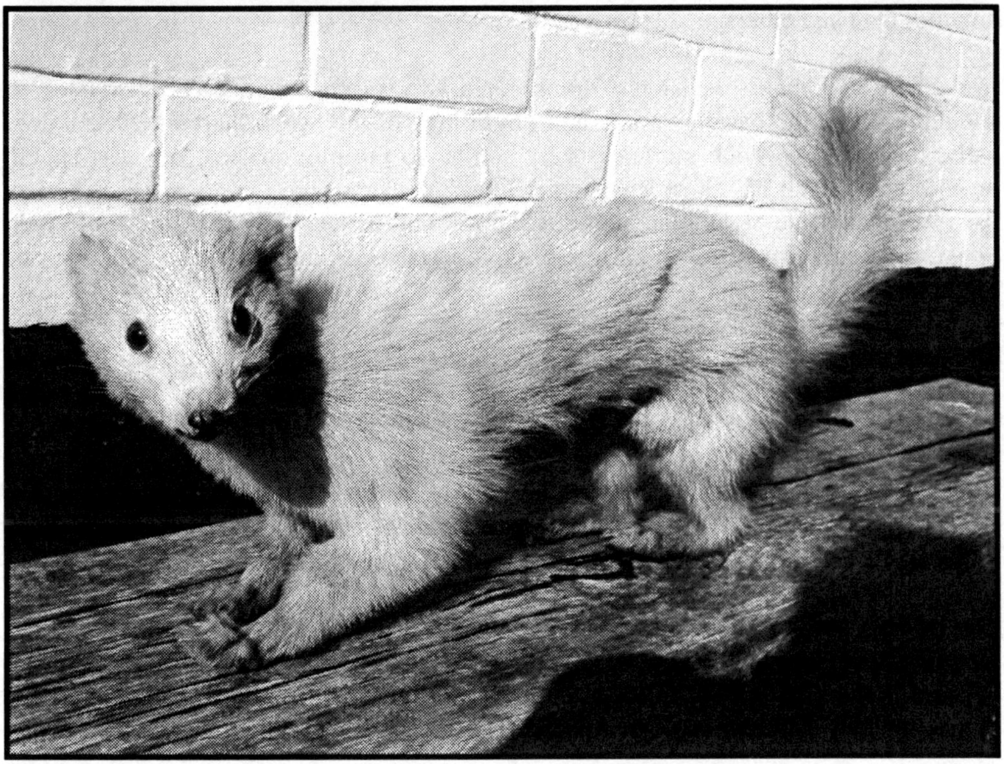

> *In Norfolk one was shot last year; and I have myself examined a fine example which was shot in Hertfordshire, within twenty miles of London, in December 1872. In Dorsetshire, the last is said to have been killed in 1804, but a specimen occurred in Hampshire about forty years ago, and another in Surrey in 1847.*
>
> *A marten is said to have been 'seen' in the Isle of Wight, and one was recorded from Cornwall by Mr. E. Hearle-Rod; but this proves, on investigation, to be an error, the specimen having been brought from North Wales, where Martens appear to be still not very rare".* [16]

This is, incidentally, the only reference we have been able to unearth to a 'Welsh' specimen turning up in Cornwall. It is interesting to compare Alston's attitudes towards the British distribution of martens with those equally fallacious figures presented by Langley and Yalden ninety years later. Both authorities, though nearly a century apart, were happy to accept records of the animals in Scotland, Wales and Ireland, but were less optimistic about their distribution in the counties of England. Interestingly, however, Alston was prepared to include some records which, in the light of the main argument of his paper, might have seemed somewhat anomalous. He did accept, however, that some authorities had allowed a greater degree of survival in some English counties than had others.

In the light of Alston's decision to combine the two species within the British Isles, we should examine the basic anatomy and physiology of the beech marten. Morphologically, the beech or stone marten is very similar to the pine marten, but it is slightly heavier in build. It has short legs, and a lighter muzzle. The ears are also smaller and narrower than those of the pine marten. The soles of the feet of *M.foina* are not as hairy either, although, unless examining a dead, very tame or anaesthetised specimen, this might be hard to ascertain.

The head and body length is 42 – 48 cm (*M.martes* 38 – 48 cm), the tail 23 – 26 cm (*M. martes* 25 – 28 cm), the height at the shoulder 12 cm (*M.martes* 15cm), and the weight between 1.3 and 2.3 kg (*M.martes* 0.5 – 1.5 kg). [19]

It ranges across most of Europe except for the Mediterranean islands (they are found on Crete), and supposedly the British Isles. It is found as far north as the southern shores of the Baltic and ranges across Asia to the Himalayas and Mongolia.

The habitats and behaviour of *M.foina* are where it differs most from *M.martes*. It is tempting to suggest that the main reason that the two species do not appear to have hybridised in the wild is that, although they occupy the same geographical area, they live in a completely different ecological niche. [20] (See Appendix Two). Its habits are more similar to those of the common polecat. It prefers more open country and is sometimes seen sitting up on its hind legs.

Here, one should note that the 1992 report of martens from Exmoor specifically noted that they were seen in open country and mentioned an animal which 'sat up' like a polecat or ferret. [21]

Unlike any other species of mustelid found in Britain (with the possible exception of some populations of badgers) *M.foina* often lives in surprisingly urban environments and has even been known to live in lofts, garages and warehouses. Like the urban fox and like some of the species of palm civet from South-east Asia, a shy and adaptable carnivore has changed its lifestyle completely to live alongside man in a new and artificial environment. [22]

The prey of the beech marten is more varied than that of the pine marten. Urban animals scavenge for rubbish as well as living off smaller urban rodents, and the animals in the more southern parts of its range eat a large proportion of amphibians. [23]

The voice is also more varied and they can make a wide variety of chattering and growling noises. They will sometimes squeal when very excited. The main external differences between the two species is that *M.foina* has a white patch or bib, rather than a cream patch on its chest. Maurice Burton's guide to the *Mammals of Britain and Europe*, (1990 edition), notes that the 'bib' is divided into left and right parts. This is undoubtedly the case, but as we have already seen the 'bib' of the pine marten can be equally bifurcated in some populations and so therefore the sight of a marten with a fragmented 'bib' is not necessarily a *bona fide* sighting of *M.foina* rather than *M.martes*. The colouration is not necessarily a definite sign either as, although the 'bib' of *M.foina* is always white, the 'bib' of *M.martes* can be such a pale fawn as to be indistinguishable from white, especially at any distance.

There are also minor osteological and dentition differences, as well as genetic differences, [24] and it is interesting to note that, although the two species co-exist over much of their range, they do not seem to interbreed. [25] (See Appendix Two). As we have seen, the naturalists of the late Victorian and early 20th Century eras were renowned for both their arbitrary 'lumping together' of disparate species and their equally arbitrary creation of new ones, simply in order to make life easier for the taxonomist.

It is an indisputable fact that, whereas a hundred and fifty years ago there were two species of marten recognised in Britain, only one has ever made it into the history books, and it also seems reasonable that utilising cryptozoological methodology, giving credence to eyewitness reports, and to the etymological evidence, the people who were actually familiar with the creatures considered them to belong to two separate species, which seems to be valuable circumstantial evidence pointing towards them being two separate species.

The history of the taxonomy of the British mustelids is an extremely complicated one and several species which are no longer recognised have been described. The Irish race of the stoat, for example, seems to be markedly different from the main body of the species (See Appendix Four). [26] The marked sexual dimorphism in the weasel led to some 19th Century observers concluding that there were, in fact, two separate species. [27] The white winter coat of the stoat prompted the inclusion of yet another separate species, the ermine, [28] into a few early handbooks on mammals. One should not create entire species on the basis of tiny physiological differences and it would be extremely unwise to consider the Irish stoat, the lesser weasel, or the ermine as separate species.

There is also reason to believe that, at least into historical times, a race of dwarf white weasels lived on the Welsh island of Anglesey, but these presently remain hidden well inside the labyrinthine archives of cryptozoology (See Appendix Four). [29]

The taxonomic status of the British beech marten is, however, a completely different one. We are not dealing with tiny differences, but with a well-known and entirely distinct species that is known across much of Europe, and until someone comes up with any convincing evidence to the contrary, I see no reason to disagree with the hypothesis that even if they are now extinct, *M.foina* was a resident of the Southwestern peninsula of the British Isles during the previous two centuries.

It seems, therefore, that whereas the natural history books claim that the pine marten was the only species ever to live in the Southwest, and that it has been extinct since the mid-19th Century, in fact, there have been three distinct species of marten (*M.martes, M.foina,* and *M.americana*) at large in the Devon countryside.

The sightings continue, but to which of the three species we have delineated the creatures belong, or whether, as seems more likely, they are hybrids between two or more of the source species, is unclear. Despite the undoubted probability of my confusing the matter even further, there is a fourth species of marten which should be discussed, when dealing with the mystery martens of Devonshire.

The sable, (*M.zibellina*) is a common animal of Northern Eurasia. It is also unfortunate enough to possess the most valuable pelt of any mustelid, [30] and, therefore, it is a common resident of fur farms. In the years before they became controlled by the legislation which now determines the workings of the industry, the Southwest was the site for a number of small, unlicensed, fur farms, from which it is highly likely that escapes took place. [31]

The animal seen by Mr. Flemming in 1988 was darker than one would normally expect a pine marten to be, and did not appear to have a 'bib' or throat patch like the three species we have described above, whose existence within the Devon ecosystem is hardly in doubt. Mr. Flemming's description was, however, a very good one...of a sable! [32]

The sable is a shorter and heavier animal than either of the species of marten described above, and its 'bib' is ill-defined and often absent. It feeds off small rodents and ground-living birds, and in the autumn will eat fruit and the seeds of the stone pine. It is mostly nocturnal but some individuals tend towards a mostly diurnal existence. It is solitary, fairly silent and climbs about in the secondary growth of coniferous trees. It makes its dens amongst rocks.

Although southern Britain is far south of its natural habitat, it is not at all inconceivable that the species could survive quite happily in Devonshire.

Here one should also note that the Cretan race of *M.foina* is said to be darker, and lacks a 'bib' of any colour. It is not impossible that a small population of *M.foina*, similarly isolated from the main body of the species, might develop similar colouration. [33]

Potentially the puzzle of the Devon martens, at least the most exciting puzzle, which is the disputed matter of *M.foina* in the region, should be relatively easy to solve. The truth, however, like Oscar Wilde once said, is never pure and seldom simple, [34] and the reality of the situation is far less hopeful.

In theory, all one should have to do is to scour the local museums and private collections until one comes across a specimen or skin that is undoubtedly a beech marten and whose provenance is certain. It appears that martens were hunted for their fur in Dorset during the 18th and 19th Centuries, and therefore one would assume that there should be a reasonable amount of research material available.

Unfortunately, not so!

In a categorical statement, smacking a little of almost religious zealotry, a representative of the mammal department of the British Museum (Natural History), vehemently denied that there are any mounted specimens of *M.foina* in their collection which had been taken anywhere in the British Isles. [35]

Mounted pine martens in the Westcountry museum collections are few and far between. Some specimens are no longer available. For example:

> "The specimen that was: 'once in the collection of the Plymouth Institution' was wild caught, its precise origin is unknown although it has been suggested that it was killed on Dartmoor". [36]

This specimen, whose origin although uncertain, constituted provenance of a degree, seems, however, to have disappeared, and no-one that we spoke to has any knowledge of its existence. [37]

The specimen in Truro Museum is of Cornish origin, but is also unprovenanced. [38] Even this is unconfirmed. Although the above reference suggests that it is a true Westcountry animal, the present staff at the museum was unable to confirm this. [39]

When we visited Truro Museum in the early summer of 1996 to take the photographs for this book, the specimen was in the store room. It is a fairly tatty specimen and so this is not particularly surprising:

The curator told us that there was no record available of how this specimen was obtained by the museum. It was obvious, however, that the specimen is fairly old, probably dating from the 19th Century, and thus was probably a wild specimen. The documentation which originally would have accompanied the animal is long since lost and, thus, it is not certain whether or not this is a true specimen of the elusive Westcountry marten, although the available evidence suggests that this is probable.

The next two specimens are interesting, especially in the light of the evidence presented elsewhere in this book, but are ultimately of no use in our quest. The specimen in the Plymouth collection was presented by H.G. Hurrell, [40] which would suggest that it was not of wild origin, and Elaine Hurrell confirmed this in writing.

A specimen in the Royal Albert Museum in Exeter is labelled as a:

> 'Continental specimen which lived wild having escaped from Hurrell's collection, and subsequently been presented to the collection by Major Vickary'. [41]

We have only been able to locate one specimen which is unquestionably of a Westcountry pine marten. This animal presently resides on display in the roof of the museum at Ilfracombe. It is fully provenanced. According to the report of the Ilfracombe Natural History Society in 1935, [42] the specimen was:

> 'Given in 1933 by Mr. W.J. Parsons of Combe Martin and was shot at Lynton many years ago'.

It is an unprepossessing and tatty specimen which is hidden away in an unimportant display by people who are unaware, or uninterested, in its uniqueness.
The hunt for the truth, or at least some semblance of the truth, continues. There must be other specimens of Westcountry pine martens hidden in private collections, and museum attics, and I am convinced that amongst them is the mounted skin which will one

day prove that the beech marten did indeed exist, and maybe still exists, in the wilder parts of the Southwest peninsula of England.

What is beyond doubt, is that some martens at least still live in the region. We have seen that in a similar scenario which we explored in great depth, when we examined the bloodlines of the Westcountry. Unfortunately, the precise state of mustelid taxonomy is even more confused than the state of felid taxonomy discussed earlier, and there is a very real possibility that even should we manage to obtain hair samples from a mounted specimen of what we believe to be a true British beech marten, that DNA tests would be inconclusive and that we would be no further forward than we are at the moment!

As a wise man once said, however, just because we are beaten before we even started, that is no reason why we should not continue the fight with as much vigour and enthusiasm as we can!

- CONCLUSION -

"Never underestimate the power of human stupidity"

Lazarus Long

The main lessons that have to be learned from the whole saga of all the disputed small carnivores in the Westcountry, is that not only do we know very little about the animals which live figuratively in our own backyard, we also have to realise that the ecosystem is ever-changing, and that the natural history of an area is seldom static and should not be treated as such.

What is static, however, is the infrastructure of the food chain and the ecosystem itself, and what is becoming more certain is that when a gap in the ecology occurs due to the decline or disappearance of a specific creature, then something else will either evolve, or grow, to replace it. When a creature is introduced into an area where it has no natural (or least extant) competitors for its place in the ecological pattern, then it will fit into that niche very neatly.

The lessons we have learned with the wildcats, pine martens and polecats (together with their more disputed relatives) are ones that the sceptics who do not believe in British mystery cats should take to heart.

We live in a totally artificial ecosystem – one with no large predators. [1] We wiped out centuries ago, our only large natural carnivores, the wolf and the bear, and nothing has ever taken their place…until the accidental introduction in the late 1970s of exotic species of big cat. Armed with this knowledge it seems only too logical that these alien predators should fill the vacant niche at the top of the food chain, and one wonders why their existence is queried by so many people.

My files include reports of animals which appear to be wolverines. [2] There is reason to suppose that these, certainly the largest and most voracious mustelid known to exist in the modern world, may be living wild in parts of Britain, including parts of the Southwest. Whether they are introduced specimens (which seems probable) or even an evolved descendant of the supposedly long extinct cave wolverine, (unlikely) remains to be seen. [3]

There *are* reports of bears from various parts of the British Isles. Many of these, as I have written elsewhere, appear to be entities of a paranormal nature, but in at least once case it seems likely that a European brown bear is living wild in woodlands, which it would have frequented many centuries ago. [4]

There have been a number of reports of arctic foxes, [5] raccoons, [6] coatis, [7] and even wolves [8] from various parts of the south of England. Even the Ministry of Agriculture, never noted for their broad-mindedness in matters cryptozoological, have admitted that it is likely that at some point the North American raccoon will become naturalised in parts of Britain, as it is across so much of western Europe. [9][10]

As our ecosystem changes, so its inhabitants change with it. Whether you accept the purely 'rational' explanations given in this book, or whether you prefer to consider some of the more abstract and surreal options that have been suggested, there is no doubt that the English countryside is home to some strange and wonderful creatures whose existence is not accepted by mainstream zoologists.

There is no doubt, at least in my mind, that even at the end of the 20th Century, in what is probably the most well explored landscape on earth, there are still mystery animals, there are still phenomena which cannot be explained using accepted scientific methodology, and that despite, or maybe even because of it all, we are still merely strangers in a strange land.

> *"The More you see*
> *The less you know"*
>
> Lao Tzu

- APPENDIX ONE -
NOTES ON THE IRISH WILDCAT

(Thanks to Richard Muirhead for much of the information included in this appendix)

The mystery of the Irish wildcat was discussed briefly in Chapter Two. For the sake of completeness, and also because the subject has only been mentioned once in recent years, [1] we decided to present the available information as an appendix to this present work.

As Karl Shuker points out, the wildcat is a common figure in Irish mythology. He lists several examples, including an archaic 9th Century poem, translated by Eugene O'Curry, and published by Oscar Wilde's father, the notorious Sir William Wilde. This poem tells of the Irish hero, Fin mac Cumhaill, who was held captive by the King of Erinn, who pledged to free him if a male and a female of every wild animal which inhabits Ireland were brought to him as a ransom. [2]

A more recent cultural reference comes in the Shane McGowan song *The Wildcats of Kilkenny*, [3] which re-tells another ancient legend about a massive battle between the wildcats of Ireland.

Despite being such a common figure in the folklore of the emerald isle, the actual zoological existence of any indigenous felid within the Hibernian zoofauna is far more problematical.

Karl Shuker noted [4] that William Andrews had noted in the mid-19th Century, that the inhabitants of the more remote glens of Kerry knew of both the pine marten and the wildcat. They had separate names for each. The pine marten was known as the 'tree cat' and the wildcat as the 'hunting cat'. Shuker goes on to list the main eye witness reports of the Irish wildcat, and presents a useful over-view of the evidence for the continuing existence of an indigenous Irish felid.

Shuker also quotes R.F. Scharff, who, in 1905, presented evidence which suggested that the Irish wildcat, whether or not it still exists, is more closely allied to the African wildcat (*F.lybica*), which, at the time Scharff was writing, was known as *Felis ocreata*. His work was concerned with skeletal fragments found in the Edenvale and Newhall caves near Ennis in County Clare.

"In examining a number of jaw fragments of cats and single teeth from these caves, I was struck by the great size of the lower carnassials, or molar teeth. Many of the individuals to whom these teeth belonged were evidently domestic cats which had strayed and had died in the caves in recent times, or whose remains had been dragged there by other carnivores. A few, however, seemed to belong to another species, and I determined to make a very careful comparison with all the available material of cats in the Dublin Museum, where, with Mr. Oldfield Thomas' kind permission, I was able to compare them with the large series of cat skulls in his charge. I likewise compared the Irish remains with those of the fossil English Wild Cat remains in the British Museum, Dr. Smith Woodward kindly granting me every possible facility for doing so. And, finally, I examined and measured the well-known jaw of a Wild Cat which is in the charge of Professor Sollas at Oxford, who gladly placed the specimen at my disposal. I have thus had opportunities for handling and critically comparing a large series of the teeth of various species of cats, both fossil and recent.

In the following table I give the measurements of the lengths of the lower carnassial teeth of Domestic Cats. In order that there should be no doubt as to the exact position where the tooth was measured, I herewith indicate the line of measurement by a dotted line on a figure representing a carnassial tooth..." [5]

Scharff continues with a detailed analysis of the findings extrapolated from the above tables. For the cryptozoologist, however, it is his conclusions linking the Irish animals with the African wildcat, that are most interesting:

"Only in two cases did this tooth reach a length of 8 mm and both of these

	Locality and Museum Register.			Sex.	Carnassial.	Carnassial to canine.	Carnassial to 1st premolar.	Upper Carnassial.	Remarks.
					m.m.	m.m.	m.m.	m.m.	
Recent in Dublin Museum.	London, ...	43.	1905	♂	7½	32	20½	10½	
	White-park Bay, Co. Antrim,	273.	1902	—	6½	27	18	10	
	loc. (?) (probably Irish), ..	79.	1902	—	6½	23	18	10	
	Dundrum, Co. Dublin, ..	——		♂	7	33½	20	10	
	Cappagh, Co. Waterford, ..	107.	1902	—	6½	30½	20	10½	
	Shot wild at Glenarm, Co. Antrim,	210.	1906	—	6½	29½	18	10	
	Shot wild at Greystones, Co. Wicklow	171.	1896	♂	8	35½	21½	abt. 11	Broken.
Fossil in Dublin Museum.	Edenvale Caves, ..	E. A. 30.	——	—	7	—	19	—	
	" ..	E. C. 230.	——	—	7	29½	19	10	
	" ..	E. C. 93.	——	—	7	27½	18	—	
	" ..	E. C. 230.	——	—	7½	30	19	10½	
	" ..	E. C. 318.	——	—	7	29	19	—	
	" ..	E. C. 87.	——	—	7	—	18	—	
	" ..	E. C. 58.	——	—	6½	—	18	—	
	" ..	E. C. 79.	——	—	7	—	18	—	
Fossil in Dublin Museum.	Newhall Caves, ..	N. H. 34.	——	—	8	34	21	—	
	" ..	N. H. 118.	——	—	8	32½	22½	—	
	" ..	N. H. 156.	——	—	8	—	21½	—	
	" ..	N. H. 102.	——	—	8	33	20	11	Whole skull preserved
	" ..	N. H. 93.	——	—	7½	28	19	—	
	" ..	N. H. 23.	——	—	7½	31	20½	—	
	" ..	N. H. 29.	——	—	7½	30½	20	—	
	" ..	N. H. 2.	——	—	7	29½	20½	—	
	" ..	N. H. 1.	——	—	7	27½	18	—	
	" ..	N. H. 86.	——	—	6½	—	17½	—	
	" ..	N. H. 102.	——	—	6½	26½	16½	—	
	" ..	N. H. 102.	——	—	6½	26	17½	—	
	Barntick Cave, ..	C. B. 7.	——	—	7	27½	19½	—	
	" ..	C. B. 3.	——	—	7	27	18	—	
	" ..	C. B. 6.	——	—	7	27	18	—	
	" ..	C. B. 11.	——	—	6½	28½	18	—	
	" ..	C. B. 2.	——	—	6½	27	19	—	
	" ..	C. B. 5.	——	—	6	26½	17	—	
Recent in Brit. Mus.	England, ..	127. f.	——	—	6½	27	18	10	
	" (tailless var.)	45. 3. 17. 10.	——	—	6½	30½	19	10	
	" ..	41. 7. 14. 46.	——	—	7	26½	18	10½	
	" ..	46. 3. 18. 8.	——	—	8	35½	22	12	
Fossil in Brit. Mus.	Gower Caves, ..	M. 95.	——	—	8	30½	21	—	
	" ..	M. 96.	——	—	6½	20½	18	—	

Tables showing Scharff's finding, first presented in 1905. 1. F. silvestris

Locality and Museum Register.		Sex.	Lower Carnassial.	Carnassial to canine.	Carnassial to 1st premolar.	Upper Carnassial.
			m.m.	m.m.	m.m.	m.m.
Recent in Dublin Museum.	Inverness, Scotland, .. 170. 1899	♂	9	33	21½	10½
	Germany, .. 322. 1904	—	9½	36	23	11½
Recent in British Museum.	Fort William, Scotland, 99. 2. 9. 1	—	7½	32½	21	10½
	Inverness, Scotland, 98. 12. 26. 1	?	8	33½	22	11
	,, ,, 4. 1. 25. 3	♀	7½	31	20	10
	,, ,, 4. 1. 25. 3	♂	7½	33	22	10½
	Caucasus, 79. 11. 15. 4. —	—	8½	34½	22	11½
	Baranxa, Hungary, 2. 6. 3. 1	♂	8	35½	22	11½
	Manonville, France, 95. 11. 9. 1	♂	8	33	21	11½

Tables showing Scharff's finding, first presented in 1905. 2. F. silvestris

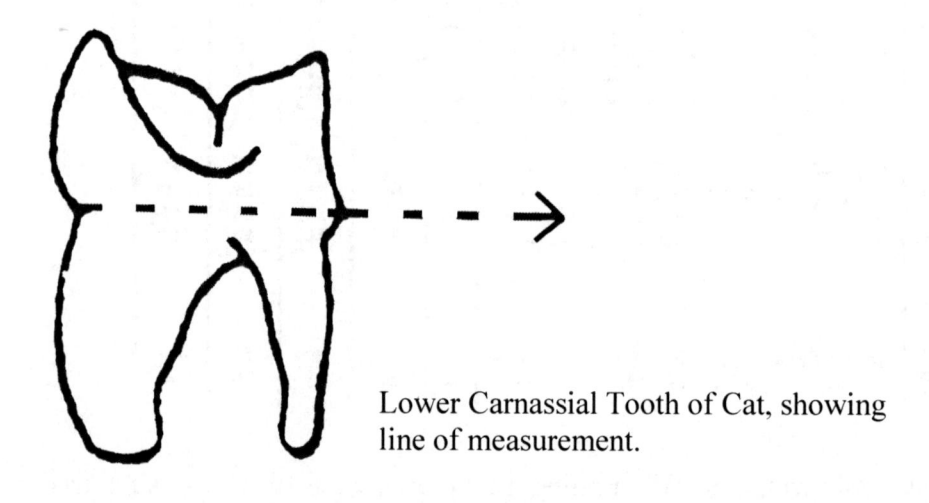

Lower Carnassial Tooth of Cat, showing line of measurement.

Locality and Museum Register.		Sex.	Lower carnassial.	Lower carnassial to canine.	Carnassial to 1st premolar.	Upper carnassial.	Remarks.
			m.m.	m.m.	m.m.	m.m.	
Recent in Dublin Museum. Sardinia,	76. 1901	♂	9	30	20½	12	
"	278. 1902	♀	8½	29½	20	11	
Abyssinia,	549. 1904	—	8½	32	21½	11½	
Recent in British Museum. Sardinia,	88. 12. 1. 1.	♂	9	31	22½	12½	
Deelfontein (Cape),	2. 12. 1. 1.	♂	9	36½	24½	12½	
" "	2. 12. 1. 3	♀	8½	35	22½	11	
" "	2. 12. 1. 2	♂	9	37	24	12½	
S. Africa, "	857. a	—	9	38½	24	12½	
Andalusia. "	2. 6. 3. 2.	♂	9	37	23	12	
"	2. 6. 3. 3.	♀	9½	34½	24	12½	
Fossil in Dublin Museum. Edenvale Caves,	E. A. 42	—	9	32	22½	—	
" "	E. C. 361	—	—	—	—	11	Upper jaw fragment.
" "	E. C. 310	—	8½	—	22	—	
Newhall Caves,	N. H. 88	—	10	36	24½	—	
" "	N. H. 118	—	8½	32½	22	—	
" "	N. H. 86	—	8½	32½	22	—	
" "	N. H. 85	—	8½	—	21½	—	
" "	N. H. 23	—	8½	33	22	—	
" "	N. H. 93	—	—	—	—	12	Upper jaw fragment.
Fossil in British Museum. Kent's Hole, Torquay,	167. 10	—	8½	33½	22½	—	
Gibraltar Caves,	—	—	9½	—	24	—	
" "	—	—	—	30	24	—	
Happaway Cave, England,	M. 5830	—	—	—	—	12½	Upper jaw fragment.
Oxford Mus. Kent's Hole, Torquay,	—	—	9½	32½	—	—	

Tables showing Scharff's finding, first presented in 1905. 3. F. silvestris *were probably old males. They were of powerful dimensions, the skull being quite as large as that of an African wildcat. One of these was shot as a wild cat in the County Wicklow. It may have been a descendant of a true wild cat, which had interbred with the domestic form. In the Gower caves of England, and in Ireland, in the Newhall caves, similar specimens have been met with, which seem to form a link between the domestic cat and the larger African wildcat, in so far as the size of the lower carnassial is concerned. The domestic cat may possibly have developed quite independently from the Wildcat in Ireland, and these intermediate stages may be the links connecting the later undoubted cave remains of domestic cats with the older ones of the genuine wWildcat"...*

From the information presented in the three tables we have reproduced above, and from the drawings reproduced in the main text of this book, which include comparisons between the jaw bones mentioned above, and those taken from mummified cats found in Egyptian tombs, it is hard not to agree with his findings.

Here, one should perhaps mention that in Victorian times, mummified cats from Egypt were imported to Great Britain and Ireland in enormous quantities to be ground up for use as fertiliser. [6] It has been suggested that these are the true origin for the discovery of so many tiny Egyptian artefacts found buried in western European fields, which have, over the years, been used as supportive evidence for some of the most preposterous fortean theories. It is not beyond the bounds of possibility that some of the jaw bones of anomalous examples of *Felis lybica* found in Western Europe may be from this prosaic source.

The enigma of the Irish wildcat remains, and like so much in that peculiar island, it seems destined to be a mystery for many years to come. Two final feline enigmas remain. The first, fittingly enough, from Scharff:

"I have met with the remains of an extremely small race of cats in the Newhall and Barntick caves. The limb bones are about the size of the ordinary Marten (Martes martes), and the lower carnassial, in one case, only measures 5.5 mm in length". [7]

This not only provides supportive evidence for the existence of two marten species in the British Isles, *M.martes* is described as the 'ordinary marten' which implies, quite strongly, that there were two species in the area. It also provides, what is, to my knowledge, the only tantalising fragment of evidence for the past existence of another Irish mystery felid.

A race of tiny Irish cats would be an exciting discovery for any zoologist. It would seem highly likely, however, that they are long since extinct, either by extermination or, more likely, by genetic dilution, a fate which, unfortunately, has probably also overtaken the cat mentioned by Karl Shuker [8] which was:

> "...of a dirty grey colour, double size of the common house cat and its teeth and claws more than proportionally larger".

Was this one of Scharff's Irish African wildcats, or something stranger and even more interesting? Maybe it was the fairy cat, the *Cait Sidh*, described by Shiels, [9] and others, given corporeal form, or maybe something wholly new to us all.

REFERENCES TO APPENDIX ONE

1. SHUKER Dr. K.P.N., *Mystery Cats of the World – from Blue Tigers to Exmoor Beasts* (Hale, London 1989) p. 84 – 89.

2. SCHARFF, R.F., 'On the former occurrence of the African Wildcat (*Felis Ocreata*) in Ireland' (*Proceedings of the Royal Irish Academy* 4.12.1905). p.1.

3. THE POGUES: *Rum Sodomy and the Lash* (STIFF Records 1986).

4. SHUKER Dr. K.P.N., *Mystery Cats of the World – from Blue Tigers to Exmoor Beasts* (Hale, London 1989) p. 85.

5. SCHARFF, R.F., 'On the former occurrence of the African Wildcat (*Felis Ocreata*) in Ireland' (*Proceedings of the Royal Irish Academy* 4.12.1905). pp.1 – 13.

6. TABOR, R. *CATS: The rise of the Cat* (BBC 1991). P.25 – 26.

7. SCHARFF, R.F., 'On the former occurrence of the African Wildcat (*Felis Ocreata*) in Ireland' (*Proceedings of the Royal Irish Academy* 4.12.1905). p.5.

8. SHUKER Dr. K.P.N., *Mystery Cats of the World – from Blue Tigers to Exmoor Beasts* (Hale, London 1989) p. 86.

9. SHIELS, Tony 'Doc', *Monstrum – A Wizard's Tale*. (FT 1987).

- APPENDIX TWO -
MUSTELID HYBRIDS

Extrapolated from *Mammalian Hybrids: A check list with Bibliography* by Annie Gray, Commonwealth Agricultural Bureaux: Farnham Royal, 1954, Second Edition 1971. (I am grateful to Karl Shuker for his help).

1. The Beech Marten, or Stone Marten (*Martes foina*)

The existence of hybrids is doubted by Frechkop (1959) but there have been reports of presumed hybrids.

* Male *M.foina* x female *M.martes*. According to Streuli (1932), a breeder succeeded in obtaining hybrids after many unsuccessful attempts, but the mother failed to rear them.

2. The Pine Marten (*Martes martes*)

* x *M.foina* (see above).
* x *M.zibellina*. Hybridisation has been alleged in the one time Soviet Union, according to Dabczewski (1958), Y.Yaxan and Y. Knorre (1964).
* x *M.putorius putorius*. Hybridisation has been alleged by K. Ackermann in 1898.

3. The Sable (*Martes zibellina*)

* x *M.martes* (see above).

4. The Stoat (*Mustela erminea*)

* Male *M.erminea* x female *M.p.furo*. According to W.A. Craft in 1938, quoting A.H. Cocks in 1899, of six presumed hybrids, one female became pregnant to a polecat but aborted almost at full term. Another mated with a male sibling produced four male and one female young. The presumed hybrids had better pelts than the ferret. They had the bright yellow throat of *M.erminea* and feet larger than those of *M.p.furo*.

5. Turkestan or Steppe Polecat (*Mustela eversmanni*)

* x *Mustela putorius furo*. Hybrids have been reported by W. Herre (1965).

6. The Weasel (*Mustela nivalis*)

* x *M.putorius furo*. Hybridisation has been alleged by K. Ackermann in 1898.

7. The Ferret (*Mustela putorius furo*)

* x *M.erminea* (see above).

* x *M.eversmanni* (see above).

* x *Mustela putorius putorius*. This is a very well-known hybrid (see notes below). The hybrids have a rapid growth rate and appear to be fully fertile. Females come on heat during their first year of life. Breeding occurs bi-annually as in the ferret. According to A.H. Cocks in 1899, the pelt is of a higher quality than that of a ferret.

* When the father is a polecat and the mother is a ferret, it is alleged that the offspring are more nervous and active than ferrets.

* *Mustela vison*. Bahlke, in 1939, failed to obtain mating between a male mink and a female ferret. According to Chang and co-workers in papers published between 1965 and 1969, a high proportion of ferret eggs could be fertilised when injected with mink sperm, especially if large numbers of sperm were injected into the ferret uterine horns. mink eggs however could not be fertilised by ferret sperm. Ferret eggs fertilised by mink sperm were able to implant but few foetuses survived more than three weeks of pregnancy. There are no records of successful births other than the one recorded in this book.

8. European Polecat (*Mustela putorius putorius*)

* x *M.martes* (see above).
* x *Mustela p.furo* (see above).

* x *Mustela vison*. The data reported by Chang and his co-workers (see above) probably also refers to this hybrid as it appears that at least some of Chang's animals were ferret x polecat hybrids (see below). Rempe (1957) states that a female polecat x ferret hybrid mated with a male mink showed signs of pregnancy or pseudo pregnancy, but no young were observed.

9. The Mink (*Mustela vison*).

* x *M.p.furo* (see above).
* x *M.p.putorius* (see above).

NOTES: For the purposes of this appendix I am using the same nomenclature as Annie Gray, who treated the ferret as a subspecies distinct from the Eurasian polecat. The notes under paragraph four are obscure enough to suggest that even she was unsure of the precise specific identity of either animal, which in turn presents supporting evidence for the theory put forward in this book that the two species are, in fact, one and the same, a conclusion corroborated by many of the above entries.

Paragraph five, however, suggests that all the animals in the polecat clan are very closely related and may, in fact, not be distinct on any level.

- APPENDIX THREE -
MAMMALS OF SOMERSET

Excerpts from *Notes of Somerset Mammals* by B.W. Tucker, taken from the 1926 volume of the *Proceedings of the Somerset Natural History Society*.

British Squirrel. *Sciurius leucourus* (Kerr)

Always present in Hollowmarsh Wood and some other woods of the Chewton Mendip district, but now rarely seen in Chewton Mendip itself, where it was common in the grounds of the Priory and Chewton House twenty years ago. A very general and widespread decrease of squirrels appears to have taken place in recent years. Notes received from the various correspondents allude to this: Seldom seen in the Bristol neighbourhood (C. Tuckett). Almost extinct at Backwell. (A.R. Robinson). Formerly common in the Hardington Mandeville district near Yeovil, but none seen for six years. (A. Vassall). Always to be seen in Butleigh Wood near Street; very scarce for two years past, but numerous again in 1925. (E. Page). Very rarely seen in the Ilminster district; the same applies to Stoke and Bickenhall. There are a few in the Orchard Portman Woods. About forty years ago they were very numerous there, but since then their numbers have been greatly reduced on account of the damage they do to the plantations. (W.H. Rendell). Unaccountably scarce in the Porlock district. (N.G. Hadden). Deliberate destruction by keepers and others in some places on account of its bird-nesting propensities, and its destructiveness to trees may be in part responsible for the observed decrease, but it will not account for it entirely. A more exhaustive enquiry on this subject is projected.

- THE SMALLER MYSTERY CARNIVORES OF THE WESTCOUNTRY -

Polecat. *Putorius putorius* **(Linn)**

A few still appear to linger in the wilder parts of the Mendip country. Keeper Brown, of Chewton Mendip, states that he trapped one in Hollowmarsh over forty years ago. Much more recently, one was shot by Mr. Reece Uphill, of Greendown, a remote hamlet on the north side of Mendip above the Harptrees, after it had killed twenty-four of his fowls. This specimen, lamentably stuffed, is in the possession of Mr. Uphill, who informed the writer in 1981 that it was killed not more than five or six years before.

Lord Waldegrave informs the writer than on 11th August, 1919 while waiting for pigeons in Eaker Hill Wood on Mendip, he had an imperfect view of 'a very dark animal of the stoat tribe', which might have been a polecat, on a low wall, 'too far away to see very distinctly and too far to shoot'. Though inconclusive, this record is of interest in conjunction with the Greendown one, the localities being not too far distant from one another.

A more problematic incident occurred in July 1916, when an animal having the appearance of a polecat made its appearance in the shrubbery of Chewton House, Chewton Mendip, where it caused some consternation by its visitations to a large rat trap, which on two or three occasions it apparently dragged for several yards in its efforts to secure the bait. It was seen in the dusk on two consecutive occasions by the writer, who waited in a tree in order to get a view of it. On the first occasion, it was observed to enter the trap and take the bait, but in this instance the lid was found to be caught. The animal disappeared after being shot at and possibly wounded by the gardener. Although it may appear unlikely that an apparent polecat in these circumstances would be a genuine wild animal rather than an escaped 'polecat-ferret', the proximity of the Mendip country and the wandering propensities with which polecats are credited should be taken into consideration before wholly rejecting the former possibility.

Pine Marten. *Martes martes* **(Linn)**

Another inconclusive, but interesting record suggest that this species may still exist in the Exmoor district. An animal believed to be a marten was seen by two members of the Ornithological Section on two separate occasions in the winter of 1924. Each time it was seen not far from Luckwell Bridge – between Wheddon Cross and Exford. On one occasion it was disturbed by hounds and on the other by a shooting party. It is quite suitable country for martens and a few might exist there for years without being observed. Further information of the occurrence of this species in Somerset or Devon is much to be desired. It is to be hoped that if the existence of the pine marten in West Somerset should be proved, all possible precautions will be taken to preserve it, as it is now almost the rarest British mammal. (Particulars communicated by N.G. Hadden).
NB. *The Somersetshire Fauna* by W. Baker (1851) notes only one marten resident in the county ...*M.foina*!

- APPENDIX FOUR -
THE IRISH STOAT, THE PYGMY WEASEL, & MUIRHEAD'S MYSTERY MUSTELIDS

(Many thanks to Richard Muirhead for his tireless research)

It is generally believed that only one species of weasel, (*M.nivalis*) and one stoat (*M. erminea*) exist in the British Isles. Within recent historical times, however, it was widely believed that there were two species of weasel and two species of stoat within these islands.

In the absence of compelling evidence to the contrary, I am prepared to concur entirely with the currently held view, but in the interests of scientific completeness, and also because, even as I write, the Centre for Fortean Zoology and its representatives are regularly approached by members of the public who believe in one or both species, I present here, the sum total of our records on the subject.

Richard Muirhead has spent some months investigating reports of dwarf weasels from various parts of the country, including the island of Anglesey and parts of Cumbria. The idea of such an animal is not particularly new. Writing in 1989 Sleeman noted:

> *"The frequent existence of a second litter, coupled with the difference in size between the sexes are the factors that give rise to stories about two types of weasels; ordinary and pygmy weasels existing side by side. In some rural areas such weasels are called 'minivers'.* [1]

Richard has discovered that these creatures are still widely believed to exist and in some areas are known as 'Squeazels'. [2] The details of the Anglesey animals are obscure, [3] but it appears that they are lighter in colour than one would expect and have been reported as being white.

Richard Muirhead writes:

> *"From a letter I received on the 28th July it appears that they live on Anglesey, in the valley area near Holyhead. They have also been reported from Cumbria, Shropshire and Yorkshire. They eat pheasant chicks and inhabit mole holes, hence the nickname of 'squeasels'. They were caught, in the 1920s and 1930s, in the areas surrounding Church Stretton, Craven Arms and Ludlow in Shropshire. They are, according to my correspondent still seen, near a farm near Llanfair near Valley. (NB LL65 2HF).*
>
> *There appear to be two types. They are of identical size but one is quite a light colour and some are much darker. The darker animals are rarer. They inhabit areas like stone walls.*
>
> *My informant saw an old one with some babies recently".* [4]

These colour variations do not seem to be consistent with those generally reported from either young or female weasels of the normal race. [5] The hunt continues.

It is generally agreed that the stoat (*Mustela erminea*) is found all over the British Isles, and unlike the weasel (or probably the polecat, although this is uncertain) is found in Ireland. Some reports, however, refer to a separate species, the Irish stoat (*Mustela hibernica*) and it is interesting to note that there seem to be several different opinions as to what exactly it is, and if in fact, it exists.

It is unclear whether or not it is believed that both the 'normal' species of stoat and the 'Irish' variety co-exist in Ireland, or whether or not only the disputed species is found.

Sleeman (1989). [5] refers to an animal the size of an ordinary weasel (Irish stoats are often referred to as 'weasels' although true weasels are confined to the mainland) on which the dividing line between the reddish upper parts and the white belly is much less well defined than on the mainland animal.

Praeger,[6] in 1950, wrote:

> *"The Irish stoat (Mustela hibernica) is now considered a different species from that found in Britain, on account of its smaller size and darker colour with less 'whitish' underneath; the lips and rims of the ears are dark, while in the English stoat they are light-coloured. Also the white winter coat, assumed by the animal in the colder parts of the range, and frequently in Britain, is scarcely ever seen.*
>
> *'Common as the animal is in Ireland' writes Thompson, 'I have never seen or heard of a white one being taken in winter. Towards the end of our most severe winters in the north, I never saw any change of fur in these animals. Yet, in the part of Scotland closest to Ireland, where the difference of climate from that on the opposite coast must be most trivial, the stoat becomes white every winter'. This active and daring little animal is common throughout Ireland, where it is usually called 'weasel' (which is 'Mustela nivalis'), and is sometimes also mistaken for the polecat (Mustela putorius); but neither of these relations of the stoat is found in Ireland. It is interesting to note that the Isle of Man is colonised by the Irish, not the English stoat (Mustela erminea stabilis)".* (see footnote)

Moffat[7] also confirms that Irish stoats are known as 'weasels'. There is some confusion here because he seems to refer to the Irish stoat as being distinct only at a sub-specific level, although other references cited are convinced that it is a distinct species.

Praeger refers several times to Thompson's classic 1856 work on *Irish Natural History*,[8] but elsewhere Thompson and others[9] collect a few records of the white winter colouration, which suggests that this variety of stoat, whether or not it is distinct at a specific level, is less prone to this mode of protective colouration than is its English counterpart. This is valuable corroborative evidence for a degree of speciation.

Thompson's book also, incidentally, contains the original reference to the Antrim beech marten specimen referred to in the main text of this book, but Thompson seems to suggest that the beech marten is by far the rarest of the two marten species living in Ireland. The final record we have of the Irish stoat is so different that, again, it appears to refer to another animal altogether. Scharff (1922) writes:[10]

---

1. I discovered an interesting codicil to this story. In 2002 when the CFZ were actively engages hunting for a giant catfish in the Martin Mere wildfowl reserve (see my book *The Monster of the Mere* for details), the head naturalist there, Pat Wisniewski, told me that the Irish stoats were also to be found at Martin Mere. This is particularly interesting, not only because the western portion of Martin Mere has a singular wildlife of its own, but because I also saw a young stoat of normal size and shape there. It appears that both races peacefully co-exist there, although, as far as I know, there is no data available on whether they interbreed.

> "Related to the Marten is the Irish stoat (Easog), commonly called 'weasel' in Ireland, an animal quite distinct from the British stoat, and even more so from the true weasel. It is unknown outside Ireland, and is much larger than the weasel. It differs from the English stoat in having the ears and upper lip dark in colour, and in so far as it rarely turns quite white in winter".

We, therefore, have a weasel-sized animal with stoat colouration, a dark, stoat-sized animal that may or may not turn white in the winter, and an animal half-way between the weasel and the stoat in size, which sometimes turns white in winter, but sometimes doesn't.

When you also consider the mystery of the Antrim beech marten and the disputed question of whether or not there is an indigenous population of polecats, the only thing that remains clear is that there is a lot of work still to be done regarding the precise speciation of the Irish mustelidae.

Other references to the Irish stoat occur in *The Irish Naturalists Journal* Volume 1, numbers 8 (p. 150 – 1), 11 (p. 219 and p. 271), Volume 2, (p. 44 and 73), and Volume 4 (p. 64).

Richard Muirhead has unearthed several other reports, which appear to refer to anomalous or in some cases, mysterious mustelids. These, I have not been able to either research or confirm, and as he has provided the rest of the material in this appendix then, again, in the interests of completeness, they should be included here.

He has a brief record of 'reddish' polecats which are reported quite regularly from several locations of the Cardiganshire plateau. Amongst other odd coloured mustelids, are an peculiar animal on display in the window of a butcher's shop in Stockbridge, Wiltshire. It was supplied by a local taxidermist. When approached for details of mustelids he had encountered, Muirhead discovered that although he didn't believe in the existence of a pygmy variety of weasel, he had come across one albino specimen, and although he had never encountered pine martens in the area, he described an animal he called a 'corn marten', which he said was now very rare, and "paler than a normal marten".

Cryptozoologists in future years may well have yet another animal to consider; the CORU marten. Richard Muirhead wrote to a Wiltshire newspaper appealing for information about the corn marten, as described above. The newspaper misprinted his request, and so an appeal went out to several thousand hapless Wiltshire men and women for information on the CORU-marten. It is frightening to think quite how many zoological mysteries may have no more substance than a spelling mistake such as this one!

Unidentified mustelid in the window of a butcher's shop in Stockbridge

- THE SMALLER MYSTERY CARNIVORES OF THE WESTCOUNTRY -

When one considers quite how many 'animals' are given considerable coverage in books on cryptozoology, purely on the basis of one uncorroborated sighting or newspaper story, the story of the 'Coru-marten' is, perhaps, of more significance than it would otherwise have seemed.

It seems appropriate that for the final animal in this book, we return to Devonshire for one final mystery animal from the pages of Richard Muirhead's notebooks. [11][12]

A 1923 report describes a mustelid which is "not a polecat", said to live in Devon in about 1900. It is described as greyish with a remarkably broad head, and Muirhead says that its identity was a "complete mystery" to the local people who encountered it!

REFERENCES TO APPENDIX FOUR

1. SLEEMAN P *Stoats and Weasels, Polecats and Martens* (1989).
2. MUIRHEAD R conversation November 1995.
3. Unnamed article in *Country Life* 1975 via R. Muirhead.
4. MUIRHEAD R pers. corr. to JD 29.7.95.
5. SLEEMAN P *Stoats and Weasels, Polecats and Martens* (1989).
6. PRAEGER R.L. *Natural History of Ireland* p.73 (1950).
7. MOFFAT C.B. *The Mammals of Ireland* (*Proceedings of the Royal Irish Academy* Vol. 44 (b) p. 61 – 128. (1938).
8. THOMPSON W. *The Natural History of Ireland* (4 Vols, Bohn, London 1856).
9. *The Irish Naturalist* (March 1895).
10. SCHARFF R.F. *Guide to the collection of Irish Animals*. (Dublin, Stationers Office; 1922).
11. MUIRHEAD R. pers. corr. to JD 21.2.95.
12. GORDON *Wildlife of Devon* (1923).

- REFERENCES -

Introduction

1. FORT, Charles, *The Book of the Damned* cited by Mr X (*Fortean Studies Vol. 1* 1994).
2. HEUVELMANS, Letter to Boris Porchnev printed in *CRYPTOZOOLOGY* 1988.
3. DOWNES, Jonathan, 'Zooform Phenomena' *SCAN NEWS #3* 1993.
4. LEVER, Sir Christopher, *Naturalised Animals of the British Isles.*
5. *Devonshire Association Mammal Report* 1979.
6. BAKER, S. et al, *Escaped Exotic Mammals in Britain.* (MAFF 1980).
7. McKEWAN, G., *Mystery Animals of Britain and Ireland* (Robert Hale, London 1986).
8. LANGLEY, P.J.W. and YALDEN, D.W., 'The Decline of the Rarer British Carnivores' ….
9. SHUKER, Dr. K.P.W., *Mystery Cats of the World – from Blue Tigers to Exmoor Beasts* (Robert Hale, London, 1989) (Chapters 1 & 2).
10. BEER, T, *The Beast of Exmoor* (Countryside Productions, Barnstaple 1988).

Chapter One: The Wildcat

1. LINNAEUS, C., *Systems Naturae* 1795.
2. SCHREBER, A, *Natural History of Mammals* 1758.
3. WILLIAMS, J., Newsfile *Animals & Men # 4.*
4. GUGGISBERG, C.A.W., *Wild Cats of the World* (1975).

5. GREEN, R., *Wild Cat species of the World* (Plymouth, Bassett Publications) 1991.
6. SHUKER, Dr. K.P.N., *Mystery Cats of the World – from Blue Tigers to Exmoor Beasts* (Robert Hale, London, 1989).
7. BOURNE, H., *Living on Exmoor* (1963).
8. WILLIAMS, J., *Op. Cit.*
9. SHUKER, Dr. K.P.N., *Op. Cit.*
10. GUGGISBERG, *Op. Cit.*
11. CFZ, 'An investigation into the Beasts of Kingsteignton' (*CFZ YEARBOOK 1996*).
12. SHUKER, Dr. K.P.N., *Op. Cit.*
13. WOOD, Rev. J.C., cited by SHUKER, Dr. K.P.N.
14. SCHARFF, Dr. R.F., (See Appendix One).
15. CFZ Records interview with Mike Davis.
16. CFZ *Op. Cit.*
17. LEVER, Sir C., *Naturalised Animals of the World* (1975).
18. LIEBERKIND, Dr. I. *Dyrenes Verden.*
19. SORENSEN, E., 'Easy as ABC' (*Animals & Men # 5*).
20. HERKLOTS, G.A.K., *The Hong Kong Countryside* (SCMP HK 1963).
21. GREEN, R., *Op. Cit.*
22. BAKER, S., *Op. Cit.*
23. BAKER, S., *Op. Cit.*
24. SHUKER, Dr. K.P.N., *Op. Cit.*
25. SHUKER, Dr. K.P.N., 'The Lovecats' (*Fortean Times*)
26. SHUKER, Dr. K.P.N., *Op. Cit.*
27. GUGGISBERG, *Op. Cit.*
28. GREEN, R., *Op. Cit.*
29. GREEN, R., *Op. Cit.*
30. HEUVELMANS, Dr. B., A Checklist of animals of interest to Cryptozoology *CRYPTOZOOLOGY Vol. 1.*
31. HURRELL, H.G., *Wildlife Tame but Free* (1968).
32. GUGGISBERG, *Op. Cit.*
33. GREEN, R., *Op. Cit.*
34. HERKLOTS, G.A.K., *Op. Cit.*
35. FRANCIS, Di, *Cat Country* (David and Charles, Newton Abbot, 1984).
36. SHUKER, Dr. K.P.N., *Op. Cit.* (Mystery Cats)
37. The precise details of the arrest were told me by the arresting PC and an official from MAFF. I have, unfortunately, lost both their names.
38. ANIMAL COUNTRY (Anglia TV 1993).
39. FRANCIS, Di., 'My Highland Kellas Cats' (Jonathan Cape 1983).
40. SHUKER, Dr. K.P.N., *Op. Cit.*
41. FRANCIS, Di, *Cat Country* (David and Charles, Newton Abbot, 1984).
42. SHARP, P., British Big Cats – a working hypothesis (*Mainly About Animals*

 # 17).
43. COBBETT, W., *Rural Rides* (London 1830).
44. VERNEY, Sir J., *Samson's Hoard* (Collins, London 1973 pp. 27 – 8).
45. HEALEY, T. & CROPPER, P., *Out of the Shadows – mystery animals of Australia* (Chippendale, Australia, Ironbark 1994).
46. SHUKER, Dr. K.P.N. British Mystery Cats – the bodies of evidence (*Fortean Studies Vol. 2*, 1995 pp. 143 – 153).

Chapter Two: The Polecat

1. BURTON, M., *A Guide to the Mammals of Britain and Europe* (TREASURE 9176).
2. *Transactions of the Devonshire Association* 1898 p. 319.
3. WINSTEAD, W., *Ferrets* (TFH Pubs 1981).
4. LANGLEY, P. & YALDEN, D., Decline of the rarer British Carnivores' (*Mammal Soc* 1977).
5. *Somerset Natural History Society* 1925 (See Appendix Three).
6. HURRELL, H.G. Mammal Report (*Transactions of the Devonshire Association Vol 111* p. 210).
7. COLLIER, W.F., cited 'Mammal Report (*Transactions of the Devonshire Association*).
8. HURRELL, H.G., (*Transactions of the Devonshire Association Vol. 97* p. 128).
9. HURRELL, H.G., as above.
10. HURRELL, H.G., (*Transactions of the Devonshire Association* 1966 p. 96).
11. HURRELL, H.G., (*Transactions of the Devonshire Association* Vol pp).
12. HURRELL, H.G., *Wildlife Tame but Free* (1968).
13. PALMER, *Mammals of the Ilfracombe District* 1940 p.3.
14. As above.
15. HURRELL, H.G., *Op. Cit.* (Tame but Free).
16. ST. LEGER-GORDON, R & HARVEY, *Dartmoor* (New Naturalist 1953, 1971 Ed).
17. LANGLEY & YALDEN, *Op. Cit.*
18. BERE R., *Wildlife in Cornwall* (1970).
19. Institute for Cornish Studies.
20. Institute for Cornish Studies.
21. Institute for Cornish Studies.
22. Institute for Cornish Studies.
23. Institute for Cornish Studies.
24. Institute for Cornish Studies.
25. Institute for Cornish Studies.

26. Institute for Cornish Studies.
27. Institute for Cornish Studies.
28. LANGLEY & YALDEN, *Op. Cit.*
29. Institute for Cornish Studies.
30. Institute for Cornish Studies.
31. Institute for Cornish Studies.
32. LEVER, Sir C., *Naturalised Animals of the British Isles* (1975).
33. BERE, R., *Op. Cit.*
34. PORTER & BROWN, *The Book of Ferrets* (1984).
35. BERE, R., *Op. Cit.*
36. JUNG, K., *Acausal Synchronicity* A concept described in many of his writings.
37. WILSON, C., *The Occult* (1975).
38. TURK, Dr. S., pers. corr. to JD/CFZ 1991.
39. DRABBLE, P. *A Book of Pets'* (1978).
40. I have, I am afraid, mislaid this reference. (Exeter University Zoology Library).
41. DRABBLE, P. *Op. Cit.*
42. DRABBLE, P. *Op. Cit.*
43. HURRELL, H.G., *Animals Tame but Free* (1968).
44. E & E 1995.
45. GRAY, A., *A check-list with Bibliography of Mammalian Hybrids* (Commonwealth Agricultural Bureaux: Farnham Royal, 1954, 2nd Edit, 1971).
46. GRAY, A., *Op. Cit.*
47. BURTON, M., *Op. Cit.*
48. LEVER, Sir C., *Op. Cit.*
49. LEVER, Sir C., *Op. Cit.*
50. GRAY, A., *Op. Cit.*

Chapter Three: The Pine marten

1. BURTON, M., *A Guide to the Mammals of Britain and Europe* (TREASURE 1976).
2. BURTON, M., *An Observers Guide to British mammals* (1958 Ed).
3. SLEEMAN, P., *Stoats and Weasels, Polecats and Martens* (1989).
4. HURRELL, H.G., *Wildlife Tame but Free* (1968).
5. LANGLEY & YALDEN, *Op. Cit.*
6. EDWARDS, M., *Fire in the Punchbowl* (Collins 1961).
7. NAISH, D., Pers. record via CFZ.
8. WHITLOCK, ?., *Wildlife of Wessex* (1976).

9. LANGLEY, P.J.W. & YALDEN, D.W., 'The decline of the rarer British Carnivores' (*Mammal Society Review* 1977).
10. *Proceedings of the Dorset Natural History and Antiquarian Field Club* 1916.
11. *Proceedings of the Dorset Natural History and Antiquarian Field Club* 1916.
12. *Proceedings of the Dorset Natural History and Antiquarian Field Club* 1952 pp. 114.
13. *Records of the Institute for Cornish Studies*.
14. TUCKER, B.W., Notes on Somerset Mammals (*Proceedings of the Somersetshire Natural History and Field Sports Society* 1925).
15. ST. LEGER-GORDON, R., *Dartmoor* (New Naturalist 1977 Ed).
16. HURRELL, H.G., 'Mammal Report' (*Transactions of the Devonshire Association Vol. 85*).
17. HURRELL, H.G., 'Mammal Report' (*Transactions of the Devonshire Association Vol. 88. p. 259*).
18. HURRELL, H.G., 'Mammal Report' (*Transactions of the Devonshire Association Vol. 104. p. 230*).
19. HURRELL, H.G., 'Mammal Report' (*Transactions of the Devonshire Association Vol. 104. p. 230*).
20. HURRELL, H.G., 'Mammal Report' (*Transactions of the Devonshire Association Vol. 106. p. 280*).
21. HURRELL, H.G., 'Mammal Report' (*Transactions of the Devonshire Association Vol. 111. pp. 210 - 211*).
22. FLEMMING, interview with CFZ 1991.
23. NETTLEY, interview with CFZ 1991.
24. HURRELL, H.G., Pine martens (Forestry Commission 1968).
25. DAVIS, M., interview with CFZ 1992.
26. ALLEN, N.V., *Exmoor's Wildlife* (1974).
27. LEVER, Sir C., *Naturalised Animals of the British Isles* (1975).
28. HURRELL, H.G., 'Mammal Report' (*Transactions of the Devonshire Association Vol. 96. p. 106*).
29. HURRELL, H.G., 'Mammal Report' (*Transactions of the Devonshire Association Vol. 97. p. 128*).
30. HURRELL, H.G., 'Mammal Report' (*Transactions of the Devonshire Association Vol. 99. p. 352*).
31. HURRELL, H.G., 'Mammal Report' (*Transactions of the Devonshire Association Vol. 104. p. 22*).
32. HURRELL, H.G., 'Mammal Report' (*Transactions of the Devonshire Association Vol. 105. p. 201*).
33. MADGE, S.C., *Records of the Institute for Cornish Studies*.
34. TURK, F.W., *Records of the Institute for Cornish Studies*.
35. MANNING, *Nature in the West-Country* (1979).

36. *Records of the Institute for Cornish Studies.*
37. PEPPER, H., (Forestry Commission records). *Conversation* 1991.
38. BURTON, M., *Guide to Mammals of Britain and Europe* (Treasure Press 1976).
39. TURK, Dr. S., pers. corr. 1991 to CFZ.
40. WMN 15.11.1977 via Institute for Cornish Studies.
41. *Records of the Institute for Cornish Studies.*
42. WMN 24.6.1983 via Institute for Cornish Studies.
43. Note attached to above press cutting in the records of the Institute for Cornish Studies.
44. ANSELL, W.F.H., Telephone conversation with JD/CFZ 1991.
45. CFZ Records via J.T. Downes.
46. CFZ Records. Note: It is always difficult when a record has to remain anonymous. I will, against my better judgement, protect the identity of my informant in this case.
47. ST. LEGER-GORDON, R., & HARVEY, *Op. Cit.*
48. HURRELL, H.G., 'Mammal Report' (*Transactions of the Devonshire Association Vol. 85.* 1953).
49. ST. LEGER-GORDON, R., & HARVEY, *Op. Cit.*
50. BLIGHT, P., Telephone conversation with JD 1991.
51. BOOT, K., Telephone conversation with JD 1991.
52. HURRELL, H.G. *Wildlife Tame but Free* (1968).
53. BOOT, K., Telephone conversation with JD.
54. TSW, Lunchtime News 18.7.92.

Chapter Four: Other Marten Species

1. LANGLEY, P.J.W. & YALDEN, D.W., *The decline of the rarer British Carnivores* (Mammal Society Review 1977).
2. LINN, I., Telephone conversation with JD 1991.
3. GRZIMEK, B., *Mammals of the World* 1985.
4. *Transactions of the Devonshire Association Vol. 111.* pp. 210 – 211.
5. BAKER, S., et al, *Escaped Exotic Mammals in Britain* (1980 MAFF).
6. BURTON, M., *Guide to Mammals of Britain and Europe* (Treasure Press 1976).
7. BOOT, K., Telephone call with JD 1991.
8. LINN, I., Telephone call with JD 1991.
9. LINN, I., Telephone call with JD 1991.
10. *Transactions of the Devonshire Association Vol. 9.* p. 325.
11. BRUSHFIELD, 'On the destruction of vermin in rural parishes.' Transactions of the Devonshire Association 1898. p. 319).

12. *Proceedings of the Somersetshire Archaeological and Natural History Society* 1851.
13. *Proceedings of the Dorset Natural History and Antiquarian Field Club* 188?.
14. The same as the above record for which my reference has been lost.
15. *Proceedings of the Dorset Natural History and Antiquarian Field Club* 1916.
16. ALSTON, E., *On the specific identity of the British Marten* (RZS 1879).
17. HILLS, D., (BMNH) Letter to JD 1991.
18. ALSTON, E., *Op. Cit.* (See Appendix Four).
19. BURTON, M., *Op. Cit.*
20. GREY, A., *Mammalian Hybrids: A Check-list with Bibliography* (Commonwealth Agricultural Bureaux; Farnham Royal, 1954, 2nd Edit. 1971) (See Appendix Two).
21. CFZ, Record cited as reference # 46 in the previous chapter.
22. CARNIVORES, Episode of 1992 BBC TV series.
23. BURTON, M., *Op. Cit.*
24. BURTON, M., *Op. Cit.*
25. GREY, A., *Op. Cit.*
26. MUIRHEAD, R., Papers on the Irish Stoat cited in Appendix Four.
27. SLEEMAN, P., *Stoats and Weasels, Polecats and Martens* (1989).
28. SLEEMAN, P., *Op. Cit.*
29. MUIRHEAD, R., cited in Appendix Four.
30. BURTON, M., *Op. Cit.*
31. Various references in the Westcountry Studies Library in Exeter.
32. FLEMMING, cited in the references to the previous chapter.
33. BURTON, M., *Op. Cit.*
34. WILDE, O., *The Importance of Being Ernest* (1894).
35. HILLS, D., Telephone conversation with JD 1991.
36. ST. LEGER GORDON, R., & HARVEY, *Op. Cit.*
37. BIRCHMORE, H., Telephone conversation with ASD October 1995.
38. Institute for Cornish Studies pers. corr. with HD 1992.
39. Truro Museum, Telephone conversation with ASD October 1995.
40. Plymouth Museum. Telephone conversation with JD 1991.
41. BIRCHMORE, H., Telephone conversation with ASD October 1995.
42. PALMER, *Mammals of the Ilfracombe District* 1937 p. 3.
43. *Transactions Royal Cornwall Institute* 1867 pp. 399 – 400.

Conclusion

1. SORENSEN, E., Letter in *Animals & Men # 4*.
2. SHUKER, Dr. K.P.N. Lecture at FT UNCONVENTION 1994.
3. CFZ, Investigation into Beasts of Kingsteignton. (*CFZ Yearbook 1996*).
4. WILLIAMS, J., 'If you go down to the woods today' *Animals & Men # 2*.
5. HURRELL, H.G., *Wildlife Tame but Free* (1968).
6. WMN, 6.2.1990.
7. WMN, 10.11.1989.
8. BROWN, Theo, *Tales from a Dartmoor Village* (1967).
9. BAKER, S. et al, *Escaped Exotic Mammals in Britain* (MAFF 1980).
10. BURTON, M., *Guide to Mammals of Britain and Europe* (Treasure Press 1976).

KEY

JD	Jonathan Downes
ASD	Alison Downes
WMN	Western Morning News
E&E	Exeter Express and Echo
CFZ	Centre for Fortean Zoology

- ACKNOWLEDGEMENTS -

This book has taken a long time to write, and an even longer time to be revised and come out in paperback. It has been fifteen years since I started to write this, and in the intervening time, a heck of a lot of water has flowed under a lot of bridges. The CFZ is no longer a tin-pot organisation with half a dozen members, but the biggest cryptozoological group in the world. Alison and I have been divorced for a decade, and I no longer live in Exeter (or keep ferrets).

Many people have helped along the way, but at the risk of leaving someone out I would like to thank the following people:

Richard Muirhead, Mark North, Graham Inglis, Richard Freeman, Darren Naish, Dr. Karl Shuker, Vonny Cornelius, Dr. Andrew Kitchener, Sally Parsons, Mary Bate, Ian Linn, Kelvin Boot, Chris Moiser, Clinton Keeling, Dr. Stella Turk, my ex-wife Alison, Dr. Frank Turk, W.F.H. Ansell, Paul Blight, Daphne Hills (snigger), Jane Bradley (RIP), Mark and Debs, Elaine Hurrell, John Allegri, the late H.G. Hurrell, Monica Edwards, Jan Williams, Keith Williams, Trevor Beer, Jonathan McGowan, my soon-to-be wife Corinna James, Tina Askew and Lisa Peach.

Jonathan Downes was born in Portsmouth in 1959, and spent much of his childhood in Hong Kong where, surrounded by age-old Chinese superstitions and a dazzlingly diverse range of exotic wildlife, he soon became infected with the twin passions for exotic zoology and the paranormal which were to define his adult life. He spent some years as a nurse for the mentally handicapped but began writing professionally in the late 1980s. He has now written over twenty books. He is also a musician and songwriter who has made a number of critically acclaimed but commercially unsuccessful albums.

In 1992 he founded The Centre for Fortean Zoology, with the aim of coordinating research into mystery animals, bizarre and aberrant animal behaviour and his own particular love of zooform phenomena (paranormal entities which only appear to be animals!)

He has searched for Lake Monsters at Loch Ness, pursued sea serpents and the grotesque Cornish Owlman - which inspired his most famous book *The Owlman and Others* - chased big cats across Westcountry moorland, and in 1998 and 2004 went to Latin America in search of the grotesque vampiric Chupacabra.

He is a popular public speaker, both in the UK and the United States, where he regularly appears at conventions talking about his many expeditions and his latest research projects.

He is also an activist for Mental Health issues, having suffered with Bipolar Disorder (Manic Depression) for many years. In 2005, after having lived in Exeter for 20 years, he moved to his old family home in Woolsery, North Devon, where he intends to establish a full-time Visitors' Centre and museum for the Centre for Fortean Zoology. Following his father's death in February 2006, he inherited the old family home and announced construction of the museum and research facility later in the year.

Other books available from
CFZ PRESS

THE OWLMAN AND OTHERS - 30th Anniversary Edition
Jonathan Downes - ISBN 978-1-905723-02-7   £14.99

EASTER 1976 - Two young girls playing in the churchyard of Mawnan Old Church in southern Cornwall were frightened by what they described as a "nasty bird-man". A series of sightings that has continued to the present day. These grotesque and frightening episodes have fascinated researchers for three decades now, and one man has spent years collecting all the available evidence into a book. To mark the 30th anniversary of these sightings, Jonathan Downes, has published a special edition of his book.

DRAGONS - More than a myth?
Richard Freeman - ISBN 0-9512872-9-X   £14.99

First scientific look at dragons since 1884. It looks at dragon legends worldwide, and examines modern sightings of dragon-like creatures, as well as some of the more esoteric theories surrounding dragonkind. Dragons are discussed from a folkloric, historical and cryptozoological perspective, and Richard Freeman concludes that: "When your parents told you that dragons don't exist - they lied!"

MONSTER HUNTER
Jonathan Downes - ISBN 0-9512872-7-3   £14.99

Jonathan Downes' long-awaited autobiography, *Monster Hunter*... Written with refreshing candour, it is the extraordinary story of an extraordinary life, in which the author crosses paths with wizards, rock stars, terrorists, and a bewildering array of mythical and not so mythical monsters, and still just about manages to emerge with his sanity intact.......

MONSTER OF THE MERE
Jonathan Downes - ISBN 0-9512872-2-2   £12.50

It all starts on Valentine's Day 2002 when a Lancashire newspaper announces that "Something" has been attacking swans at a nature reserve in Lancashire. Eyewitnesses have reported that a giant unknown creature has been dragging fully grown swans beneath the water at Martin Mere. An intrepid team from the Exeter based Centre for Fortean Zoology, led by the author, make two trips – each of a week – to the lake and its surrounding marshlands. During their investigations they uncover a thrilling and complex web of historical fact and fancy, quasi Fortean occurrences, strange animals and even human sacrifice.

**CFZ PRESS, MYRTLE COTTAGE,
WOOLFARDISWORTHY BIDEFORD,
NORTH DEVON, EX39 5QR
w w w . c f z . o r g . u k**

Other books available from
CFZ PRESS

ONLY FOOLS AND GOATSUCKERS
Jonathan Downes - ISBN 0-9512872-3-0

£12.50

In January and February 1998 Jonathan Downes and Graham Inglis of the Centre for Fortean Zoology spent three and a half weeks in Puerto Rico, Mexico and Florida, accompanied by a film crew from UK Channel 4 TV. Their aim was to make a documentary about the terrifying chupacabra - a vampiric creature that exists somewhere in the grey area between folklore and reality. This remarkable book tells the gripping, sometimes scary, and often hilariously funny story of how the boys from the CFZ did their best to subvert the medium of contemporary TV documentary making and actually do their job.

WHILE THE CAT'S AWAY
Chris Moiser - ISBN: 0-9512872-1-4

£7.99

Over the past thirty years or so there have been numerous sightings of large exotic cats, including black leopards, pumas and lynx, in the South West of England. Former Rhodesian soldier Sam McCall moved to North Devon and became a farmer and pub owner when Rhodesia became Zimbabwe in 1980. Over the years despite many of his pub regulars having seen the "Beast of Exmoor" Sam wasn't at all sure that it existed. Then a series of happenings made him change his mind. Chris Moiser—a zoologist—is well known for his research into the mystery cats of the westcountry. This is his first novel.

CFZ EXPEDITION REPORT 2006 - GAMBIA
ISBN 1905723032

£12.50

In July 2006, The J.T.Downes memorial Gambia Expedition - a six-person team - Chris Moiser, Richard Freeman, Chris Clarke, Oll Lewis, Lisa Dowley and Suzi Marsh went to the Gambia, West Africa. They went in search of a dragon-like creature, known to the natives as `Ninki Nanka`, which has terrorized the tiny African state for generations, and has reportedly killed people as recently as the 1990s. They also went to dig up part of a beach where an amateur naturalist claims to have buried the carcass of a mysterious fifteen foot sea monster named 'Gambo', and they sought to find the Armitage's Skink (Chalcides armitagei) - a tiny lizard first described in 1922 and only rediscovered in 1989. Here, for the first time, is their story.... With an forward by Dr. Karl Shuker and introduction by Jonathan Downes.

BIG CATS IN BRITAIN YEARBOOK 2006
Edited by Mark Fraser - ISBN 978-1905723-01-0

£10.00

Big cats are said to roam the British Isles and Ireland even now as you are sitting and reading this. People from all walks of life encounter these mysterious felines on a daily basis in every nook and cranny of these two countries. Most are jet-black, some are white, some are brown, in fact big cats of every description and colour are seen by some unsuspecting person while on his or her daily business. 'Big Cats in Britain' are the largest and most active group in the British Isles and Ireland This is their first book. It contains a run-down of every known big cat sighting in the UK during 2005, together with essays by various luminaries of the British big cat research community which place the phenomenon into scientific, cultural, and historical perspective.

CFZ PRESS, MYRTLE COTTAGE,
WOOLFARDISWORTHY BIDEFORD,
NORTH DEVON, EX39 5QR
w w w . c f z . o r g . u k

Other books available from
CFZ PRESS

ANIMALS & MEN - Issues 1 - 5 - In the Beginning
Edited by Jonathan Downes - ISBN 0-9512872-6-5

£12.50

At the beginning of the 21st Century monsters still roam the remote, and sometimes not so remote, corners of our planet. It is our job to search for them. The Centre for Fortean Zoology [CFZ] is the only professional, scientific and full-time organisation in the world dedicated to cryptozoology - the study of unknown animals. Since 1992 the CFZ has carried out an unparalleled programme of research and investigation all over the world. We have carried out expeditions to Sumatra (2003 and 2004), Mongolia (2005), Puerto Rico (1998 and 2004), Mexico (1998), Thailand (2000), Florida (1998), Nevada (1999 and 2003), Texas (2003 and 2004), and Illinois (2004). An introductory essay by Jonathan Downes, notes putting each issue into a historical perspective, and a history of the CFZ.

THE BLACKDOWN MYSTERY
Jonathan Downes - ISBN 978-1-905723-00-3

£7.99

Intrepid members of the CFZ are up to the challenge, and manage to entangle themselves thoroughly in the bizarre trappings of this case. This is the soft underbelly of ufology, rife with unsavory characters, plenty of drugs and booze." That sums it up quite well, we think. A new edition of the classic 1999 book by legendary fortean author Jonathan Downes. In this remarkable book, Jon weaves a complex tale of conspiracy, anti-conspiracy, quasi-conspiracy and downright lies surrounding an air-crash and alleged UFO incident in Somerset during 1996. However the story is much stranger than that. This excellent and amusing book lifts the lid off much of contemporary forteana and explains far more than it initially promises.

GRANFER'S BIBLE STORIES
John Downes - ISBN 0-9512872-8-1

£7.99

Bible stories in the Devonshire vernacular, each story being told by an old Devon Grandfather - 'Granfer'. These stories are now collected together in a remarkable book presenting selected parts of the Bible as one more-or-less continuous tale in short 'bite sized' stories intended for dipping into or even for bed-time reading. `Granfer` treats the biblical characters as if they were simple country folk living in the next village. Many of the stories are treated with a degree of bucolic humour and kindly irreverence, which not only gives the reader an opportunity to re-evaluate familiar tales in a new light, but do so in both an entertaining and a spiritually uplifting manner.

FRAGRANT HARBOURS DISTANT RIVERS
John Downes - ISBN 0-9512872-5-7

£12.50

Many excellent books have been written about Africa during the second half of the 19th Century, but this one is unique in that it presents the stories of a dozen different people, whose interlinked lives and achievements have as many nuances as any contemporary soap opera. It explains how the events in China and Hong Kong which surrounded the Opium Wars, intimately effected the events in Africa which take up the majority of this book. The author served in the Colonial Service in Nigeria and Hong Kong, during which he found himself following in the footsteps of one of the main characters in this book; Frederick Lugard – the architect of modern Nigeria.

**CFZ PRESS, MYRTLE COTTAGE,
WOOLFARDISWORTHY BIDEFORD,
NORTH DEVON, EX39 5QR
w w w . c f z . o r g . u k**

THE CENTRE FOR FORTEAN ZOOLOGY

The Centre for Fortean Zoology is the world's only professional and scientific organisation dedicated to research into unknown animals. Although we work all over the world, we carry out regular work in the United Kingdom and abroad, investigating accounts of strange creatures.

THAILAND 2000
An expedition to investigate the legendary creature known as the Naga

SUMATRA 2003
'Project Kerinci'
In search of the bipedal ape Orang Pendek

MONGOLIA 2005
'Operation Death Worm'
An expedition to track the fabled 'Allghoi Khorkhoi' or Death Worm

Led by scientists, the CFZ is staffed by volunteers and is always looking for new members.

To apply for a **FREE** information pack about the organisation and details of how to join and receive our quarterly journal, plus information on current and future projects, expeditions and events.

Send a stamp addressed envelope to:

THE CENTRE FOR FORTEAN ZOOLOGY
MYRTLE COTTAGE, WOOLSERY,
BIDEFORD, NORTH DEVON EX39 5QR.

or alternatively visit our website at: w w w . c f z . o r g . u k

Lightning Source UK Ltd.
Milton Keynes UK
UKOW032339070412

190290UK00001B/41/A